MAKING
HORSES
DRINK

How to Lead and Succeed in Business

ALEX HIAM

Includes a note from KEN BLANCHARD
Co-author of *The One Minute Manager* and *Whale Done!*

EP
Entrepreneur®
Press

Editorial Director: Jere L. Calmes
Cover Design: Beth Hanson-Winter
Composition and Production: Eliot House Productions

This publication is designed to provide accurate and authoritative information in regard to the subject matter covered. It is sold with the understanding that the publisher is not engaged in rendering legal, accounting, or other professional services. If legal advice or other expert assistance is required, the services of a competent professional person should be sought.
—From a Declaration of Principles jointly adopted by a
Committee of the American Bar Association and
a Committee of Publishers and Associations

Library of Congress Cataloging-in-Publication
Hiam, Alexander.
    Making horses drink: how to lead and succeed in business/by
Alexander Hiam.
        p.   cm.
    Includes index.
    ISBN 1-891984-50-0
        1. Leadership. 2. Employee motivation. 3. Success in business. I. Title.
    HD57.7 .H52 2002
    658.4'09—dc21   2002019155

Printed in Canada

10 09 08 07 06 05 04 03 02   10 9 8 7 6 5 4 3 2 1

Contents

A Note to the Reader

I ask people all the time "Would you rather be magnificent or ordinary at work?" Everyone chooses magnificent. I don't get anyone choosing ordinary. And yet, do we get some ordinary behavior at work? Sure we do. I think that's because of the way we treat people. We accent the negative. People want to develop, they want to make a difference, they want to get involved—and they want to be magnificent!

Business leaders can have a wonderfully positive impact on their employees and their organizations, often through simple deeds and words. People don't mind being challenged to perform better if their request comes from a caring heart.

In this book, Alex collects hundreds of examples and tips to inspire readers who wish to expand their leadership repertoire. The quest for new ideas and actions is an energizing one. This book is sure to inspire you and renew your belief in the limitless potential of people to achieve what they set their hearts on doing.

—Ken Blanchard, co-author,
The One Minute Manager and *Whale Done!*

Introduction
Horse Power

Imagine a stable full of stalls. Each of the stalls has a horse in it, and those horses are powerful beasts. (After all, that's where the term "horsepower" comes from.) But most of the time, those horses are doing little or nothing. Left to its own devices, a horse likes to stand around and munch hay. It doesn't look for heavy carts to pull, races to run, high fences to jump, steer to rope, or people to give rides to.

A stable represents a lot of potential energy that isn't much use to anyone until it's harnessed to some worthwhile goal and encouraged to work under good leadership.

Organizations are like that too. They may have a great bunch of people on their payroll, a winning "stable" if you will. But without the right touch on the reins, the business produces little more than a stable full of horses. (In fact, like a stable, it actually *consumes* in its resting state. Anything it produces is waste product, to put it politely.)

This is really two books combined, each offering a unique view of the leadership challenge. The first book explores leadership through a story and business leaders' reactions to it. The second book collects hundreds of applications, tips, and examples to help leaders spur their organizations on to peak performance.

Every horse needs a rider. Enter management. So what is management's role?

Sometimes it seems like management's role is to force those lazy horses and organizations to get out and do something to earn their keep. The "dumb beasts" need to be sufficiently controlled so that management can tug the reins or dig them in the side with the spurs or, if necessary, occasionally crack the whip to get them going in a useful direction.

But we know that is not the way to get a horse or a business to do great work. *You can't force a horse to win.* Horses are big and strong—that's what makes them so valuable to their riders. But as a consequence of their strength, you can't actually make them do much of anything they don't agree to do.

As the old saying goes, you can lead a horse to water but you can't make it drink. When it comes to the kinds of actions leaders seek from their employees in business today, the same holds true. A controlling, directive style might get you obedience, discipline, and compliance—but leaders want different behaviors from their employees: initiative, collaboration, enthusiasm, teamwork, problem-solving. These are not things you can *make* anyone do. They arise from within, they are the products of *internally* motivated employees. Perhaps you can inspire and support such behavior, but you cannot order or demand it.

What do you do if you want the *fastest* horse, if you want to *win* the race, not just trot around the ring until quitting time? That is what this book is about.

Peter Schutz is an American executive who returned to Germany (many years after fleeing as a child to escape the Nazi regime) to turn an ailing Porsche A.G. around. How did he do it? By applying a philosophy he calls "extraordinary results with ordinary people." Because, as he points out, winning companies may have good people in them, but they do best when their managers find ways of inspiring those people to *work better and achieve more* than they otherwise might.

I had a chance to work with Peter recently and was deeply impressed by how simple and impressively *human* his approach is. He exemplifies a leadership style that inspires others to reach deep into themselves and produce extraordinary results. People who have worked with him often describe that experience as the high point of their careers, and they recall having a great deal of *fun*—as well as achieving significant *results*. This is a two-sided legacy I think every executive would do well to achieve.

The elements of extraordinary success in many such cases are subtle and sometimes surprising. If you turn to the table of contents, you'll see my summary of them. Each of the ten chapters corresponds to a factor that I believe highly successful leaders use. Each is an important element of winning any horse race you wish your organization to enter. While they may seem like common sense, knowing when and how to apply each is a challenge.

Think of the horse as the great body of people who make up your business or whatever other sort of group you wish to lead. It represents your workforce and the potential that workforce has to produce extraordinary results. (Or instead, to balk and buck and shy and run away and fight the reins and refuse to drink and otherwise cause no end of trouble.) You might think of yourself as trying to climb atop that horse and stay in the saddle as you try to influence its performance and win the race.

There are many things you can do to awaken enthusiasm and nurture a thirst for success in your organization. If you haven't done at least one thing toward this goal today, try opening this book in the middle and seeking a story that inspires you to leadership action.

"Half the failures in life arise from pulling in one's horse as he is leaping."
—JULIUS AND AUGUSTUS HARE
(*GUESSES AT TRUTH*, 1827)

> **"I**f you keep on doing what you've always done, you will keep on getting what you've always gotten."
>
> —POPULAR SAYING

> **W**hich horses win races—the ones the jockey whips the hardest, or the ones who enjoy running the most?

How do you win that leadership race to achieve business success through the efforts of others? It is a question as old as the urge to achieve itself. In this book I am going to explore the answers, first by sharing a fable that many people find helpful as they wrestle with the challenges of leadership. Then we will move into the "real world" of work by examining hundreds of stories, tips, and examples. This combination of storytelling and real-world techniques helps translate insight into hands-on, daily actions that can make a real difference in the leader's life and the lives of his or her people and their workplace.

To lead people, you must first have opportunities to interact with them. That's why I like actions that increase the *overlap* between managers and employees. (For instance, Bob Nelson suggests in *1001 Ways to Energize Employees* that you make a point of getting together with employees you don't usually interact with, and also enter and exit the workplace through different paths each day, taking a little time to interact with employees you see along the way.)

Some days I feel like my own organization runs faster and smarter because I am in the saddle, but other times I worry that I am just adding weight or slowing it down. My quest as a small business owner and also a trainer and advisor to many other managers is to try to *maximize the rider's contribution* to the race. Researching and writing these books has helped me enhance my own understanding of that fascinating challenge, and I hope you enjoy the reading nearly as much as I have the writing.

Have a good ride!

LEGAL PERSPECTIVE

An Ounce of Prevention!

The legal perspective on management is often overlooked in books on leadership. It shouldn't be. There are a great many ways in which legal issues end up costing U.S. employers time, money, and effort that could have been far better spent.

Most workplace leaders do not mean to take legal risks, but do so anyway out of a lack of understanding of the often-difficult issues. Good intentions do not make a good legal defense! Because you want to make sure that while you're trying to do good you don't do harm by accident, I have invited Nancy L. O'Neill, Esq. of the national labor and employment law firm Jackson Lewis to contribute a legal perspective.

You will find her Legal Perspective features throughout the book where the content suggested something to Nancy she felt readers ought to know about. I am very pleased to be able to include this "ounce of prevention" and found I learned a good deal myself in the process.

There are plenty of legal issues to trip us up in our leadership ride, so I recommend you get good legal advice about management issues as often as you can.

Is it bad for business when your employees horse around—or is this perhaps a sign of energy, enthusiasm, and team spirit?

"I think almost everything comes down to people. That is probably the most important lesson I have learned. Management 101, but it is very important."

—STEVE CASE,
CHAIRMAN, AOL
TIME WARNER INC.

BOOK 1

A Leadership Fable
The Horse Who Wouldn't Drink

WHAT CAN WE LEARN ABOUT SUCCESSFUL LEADERSHIP FROM A
STORY ABOUT A BOY AND HIS HORSE?

A

The Gathering

"Like they always say, you can lead a horse to water but you can't make it drink," the young woman said. She was one of a dozen people attending a leadership workshop. They were talking during a break about their experiences as entrepreneurs and business managers.

"I know what you mean," another participant agreed, "but I wonder if I am trying to do just that. Did you ever hear the definition of insanity as 'doing the same thing over and over and expecting to get different results?' Sometimes I think that's me at work."

"I have 25 employees in my office, and you wouldn't believe the attitude problems some of them have," a third person chimed in. "I've got people who have been there for years and don't care *what* I say. They just do their jobs the way they've always done them and duck any extra work. Trying to get them excited about new ideas is like pulling teeth."

"Or like trying to get a horse to drink water when it doesn't want to," another manager added. "I've been in supervision for quite a few years now and I often find it frustrating. It's easy to start feeling like it's 'us against them' sometimes."

"I run my own business," another said, "and I have a hard time finding employees who care as much as I do. Just the other day, one of our customers had a problem and instead of solving it, my employee said it was quitting time and went home. I had to take over and help the customer or we would have lost their business."

"My problem is that I don't feel my employees communicate very well with me or even with each other," added a young executive. "For instance when I held a meeting to discuss a new project the other day, a couple of the employees talked too much and the others didn't contribute at all. Later on I found there was a big problem with the project that nobody had bothered to mention."

"So what can we do about our employee concerns?" the first manager asked. "Get tough? Sometimes I think I'm not tough enough to keep my people in line."

"But is that what you really want—to keep your people *in line*?" asked an older woman who had been sitting quietly in the corner listening to the discussion. "Obedience is one thing and great performances are quite another. Tough managers may maintain control, but do they get great performances from their employees?"

"That's definitely an issue," a man agreed. "We need our people to take initiative, to solve problems, and to work well together as a team. I don't think I'm going to get those sorts of behaviors by being a drill sergeant. But I'm not sure what the alternative is. If I ignore them I know I won't get the great performances I need either. There must be some secret to it."

"Maybe there *is* a secret," the older woman said with a smile, "or perhaps many secrets. If we each share our best ideas and try ideas we learn from each other, maybe we can make some real progress. And your asking about a 'secret' also reminds me of a story I once heard that I think might help. Do you want me to share it with you?"

The supervisors and entrepreneurs around her all nodded their heads eagerly.

"It may take a little while for me to tell it," she said. "Why don't you make yourselves comfortable?" So they pulled chairs into a circle and settled in to listen to her tale.

The story, to their surprise, was not about a modern business at all. It was about one of the oldest sorts of businesses in the world— a small farm, the family that ran it, and the workhorse whose help they depended upon to complete their many chores. Here is the story she told them.

B

The Story

*I*t was a hot, dusty morning in an ancient land, far away from here. A land of farms and forests, of thatch-roofed cottages and arched stone bridges over deep, dark streams.

Out of one of those cottages came a young boy. He strode across the yard to a small stable and opened the creaking wood door. In this stable lived his family's pride and joy, a newly purchased workhorse with rippling muscles, flowing black mane and tail, and the deepest black eyes the boy had ever seen.

The boy was a little afraid of this horse, but he was also proud to be put in charge of it for the spring plowing. His family were farmers, and in addition to the handsome new horse, their other great treasure was a plot of rich farmland across the river.

The boy's father had been called away to the nearest city on urgent business, leaving the boy in charge of plowing for the first time. The rains would come any day now, and the boy knew he must make haste to prepare the fields for planting.

The boy nervously reached for the harness and, standing on tip toes, placed it carefully on the horse. The horse whinnied and shook its head but finally accepted and they walked out of the yard and down the dusty road together.

When they came to where an old stone bridge arched over the river, the boy led the horse down a path to a sandy cove beneath the bridge. Here it was customary for the villagers to water their animals, and the boy knew he needed to water the horse before they started the plowing, for his father had warned him that he must not work the horse all day in the hot sun unless it drank its fill.

They had to wait a few minutes while an older farmer watered his team of mules. The mules waded into the water thirstily and buried their noses in it while the farmer leaned down to fill his leather flask and wash his dusty face and hands in the refreshing water.

When the old man and his mules had left, the boy led his handsome horse to the bank and released the reins. But the horse just stood there.

The boy leaned over and drank from the water himself, for he was thirsty and did not think he could go on without a drink. Then he said to the horse, "You better drink up now because there isn't any water at the field and we're going to be there all day."

The horse just looked at him.

The boy scooped up some water in his hands and put it under the horse's nose, but the horse ignored it.

Then a harsh voice hailed the boy from the road above. "Hey, are you going to be there all day? I've got a horse to water and a field to plow too. Come on up so I can have my turn!"

The boy said, "Sorry, I'll just be a minute. My horse doesn't want to drink."

He grasped the horse's reins and tried to pull its head down toward the cool water. But as hard as he pulled, the horse just pulled back harder. The boy was not strong enough to force its head down. Finally he gave up in frustration and led the horse back up to the road, across the bridge, and into the broad fields on the far side. They walked for another 15 minutes or so until they reached his father's landholding—a huge rectangle of weedy dirt running up to the edge of the woods. Just as they reached it, they passed a farmer who was busy plowing the plot next to theirs. He greeted the boy with a wave, complimented him on the handsome new horse, and said, "I hope you watered that horse well, young man. It's a hot day and your father wouldn't want anything to happen to it while he's gone!"

"Yes sir," the boy mumbled, wondering what he ought to do. But the horse accepted the harness and plow without complaint, and soon was plowing the first furrow with ease.

However when the horse got to the end of the row, the boy could not get it to turn all the way around and start another furrow beside the first one. When he tugged on the reins the horse put its ears back, dug its hooves into the dirt, and refused to budge. Nothing the boy did would move it. Finally he lost his temper and started shouting at his horse.

"Whoa there young man, what seems to be the trouble?" It was the farmer from the neighboring field, who had noticed the boy's difficulties and had come over to help.

"I can't get this horse to turn around and plow the next furrow," the boy explained.

"Hmm," the old farmer said, "let me have a look." He stroked his long gray beard, then walked all around the horse examining it closely. "Seems perfectly healthy," the farmer finally concluded. "I can't see what the problem could be. Did you water him well before you took him over the bridge?"

"Well, as a matter of fact sir," the boy admitted, "I couldn't get him to drink. He didn't seem to be thirsty."

"That must be the problem," the farmer concluded, nodding his head wisely. "He needs water before he can do any more work in this weather. You'd best bring him back to the river and try again."

"But it's a 15 minute walk. If I take him there now I'll lose at least a half hour of plowing time," the boy complained. "How will I ever get this field done?"

"You won't get anything done if you just stand there playing tug of war with your horse," the old man replied with a laugh. "Better late than never."

So the boy unhitched the horse from the plow and led it back down the dusty road, over the old stone bridge, and down the winding path to the watering place again.

The horse stood there, ignoring the water.

In desperation, the boy left his horse tethered to a sapling on the bank of the river and ran home to ask his grandmother what to do. He found her hanging up the washing on a line in back of the cottage. When he explained his problem, she pointed out that his father had watered the horse in its stall the day before by bringing water to it in a bucket. "Maybe it only likes to drink out of buckets," his grandmother suggested. So the boy carried a wooden bucket back to the river, filled it with water, then placed it in front of the horse.

The horse looked at him. It looked at the bucket. Then it looked away and closed its eyes.

The boy said, "Come on now, drink the water so we can finish the plowing."

The horse kicked the bucket over, spilling the water in the sand.

The boy's face flushed and his temper rose, but he calmed himself and refilled the bucket. Then he placed it in front of the horse and stood back.

Without even looking down, the horse casually turned the bucket over once more. The water sloshed into the dirt and splashed over the boy's feet, leaving a muddy stain on his sandals and pants.

The boy grabbed the bucket, scooped it full, then strode angrily up the bank until he was standing high enough that he could look the horse in the eye. He shouted, "You're going to drink whether you want to or not!" and splashed some of the water at the horse.

The horse narrowed its eyes and put its ears back as the cold water drenched its face and dribbled through its mane, then ran down leaving shiny black streaks on its dusty forelegs.

The boy was about to shout at it again when he was interrupted by the sound of bubbling laughter.

He looked around but could see no one.

The laughter continued, rising and falling like water lapping over rocks in a stream.

Embarrassed, the boy called out "Who's there?" but no one answered. The boy looked around nervously, thinking someone must have been watching him from a hiding place nearby. But he could find no one in the bushes or under the bridge, and now the laughter had stopped and all he could hear was the river against the pilings of the bridge.

The boy sighed and said, "Okay, you win...this time. But tomorrow I'll find a way to make you drink. Just you wait and see!" Then he led the horse back to its stable, where he brushed it down, gave it hay and oats, fetched a bucket of water from the well and set it inside the stall just in case the horse decided to drink during the night.

Much to his surprise, the horse buried its nose in the bucket right away and drank until the water was gone.

"But, but..." the boy sputtered in indignation. "Why wouldn't you drink at the river? Why wouldn't you drink when I wanted you to plow the field? Why do you only drink now, when I've brushed you and fed you and put you away for the day?"

The horse just eyed him quietly, its tail swishing from side to side.

Finally the boy left the horse in its stall and went into the cottage, where his grandmother was beginning to prepare for dinner. "What are you doing back so early?" she asked. "Did the plowing go so well that you can take the afternoon off?"

"Not exactly," he said, and then told her everything that had happened since he'd last spoken with her. "And the strangest thing of all," the boy added, "was that someone was laughing at me from under the

bridge. I had the feeling someone was watching me the whole time, but I couldn't see anyone."

She paused in her work and wiped her hands on her apron. "You say it was a musical laugh?" she asked.

"Yes. At first I thought it was just the river lapping the bank."

"Well, I'll be..." his grandmother said. "Now isn't that amazing!"

"What's amazing?" the boy asked.

"You must have heard the spirit of the river," she continued. "When I was young they used to tell stories of a magical river spirit who inhabited the water under the old stone bridge. Sometimes she would appear to ask travelers riddles, and if they couldn't answer, they would be swept off the bridge and never seen again. Other times she would rise up out of the river to help people in their time of need. People used to throw a coin into the river and ask the spirit for advice. But I haven't heard of anyone seeing her for a long, long time."

The boy was much troubled by his grandmother's stories and had difficulty falling asleep that night. As a consequence he woke late, long after sunrise when the farmers usually went out to plow their fields. His grandmother gave him a biscuit and a cup of warm milk, then hurried him out to start his work.

He was surprised to find that the horse was not in its stable where he had left it, but was grazing on the stubble of grass behind the stable instead, the door to its stall mysteriously ajar. He hoped that the horse had not figured out how to unlatch its stall door. It wouldn't do to have it coming and going whenever it wanted to. What if it ran away?

The boy sighed as he took up the reins and once again led the horse down the road toward the old stone bridge.

He did not feel very good.

He was worried about the horse and the field and what would happen if he could not get the horse to drink. He walked with heavy steps, his eyes cast down at the ground before him and his thoughts weighing on his mind. He didn't notice the warm scent of spring flowers or the happy tinkle of birdsong. He just trudged along, his feet shuffling in the dust.

Then something gold glittered in the dirt at his feet.

He stopped, and the horse stopped quietly behind him. He leaned over and brushed the dirt aside. He picked the thing up.

It was a heavy gold coin of a kind the boy had never seen before. It looked dented and old, and very valuable. It had some writing the boy could not decipher on one side, along with a picture of a bridge arching over a river. On the other was a picture of a horse running at top speed.

Pleased with his luck, the boy began to walk again, clutching the coin tightly in one hand and holding the reins with the other.

Soon they reached the winding path down to the watering hole. When they were by the river once again, the boy stood close beside his horse and whispered to it, "I'm sorry I lost my temper yesterday. Now please, please, won't you drink some water so we can go and do the plowing? It's very important to me."

The horse twitched its ears and whinnied, then it nuzzled its nose into the boy's hand.

And the coin slipped out of his hand.

It rolled down the bank, bounced on a rock, arced gracefully into the air, splashed into the river, and sank out of sight beneath the dark water.

The boy leapt down the bank after it and, wading out, tried to feel for it on the bottom. But the ground angled steeply down and the current was strong. He soon realized that the coin must have been washed down to the deep water beneath the bridge.

The boy turned angrily toward the horse and was about to say something, but bit his tongue. What was the point? It was only a dumb animal, it didn't know what it had done.

Sadly, he grasped the horse's reins, tugged its head around, trudged up the winding path onto the road, and began to cross the bridge. "I guess you'll just have to plow today without any water," he said to the horse, "since we've got a lot of work to do and I still haven't figured out the secret of making horses drink."

"Are you sure that's a good idea?" a soft voice answered him.

"Who's that?" the boy said in surprise, stopping in the middle of the bridge and looking around at the empty road. "Who's talking to me?"

"I thought you were talking to me," the soft voice continued, seeming to bubble up from the very stones beneath his feet. "It was you who summoned me, wasn't it?"

"Summoned? Summoned who?" the boy said nervously, remembering his grandmother's superstitious tales.

"Summoned me with your gold coin," the voice continued. "A very valuable token indeed. You must be in great need to spend so lavishly on advice."

"But wh-who are you and where are you?" the boy stammered, increasingly alarmed.

"You don't need to be afraid. Just lean over the side of the bridge and you'll see me."

"But my grandmother told me that people used to be dragged into the water and drowned by a river spirit," the boy said nervously.

"People are often afraid of wisdom," the voice said with a laugh like a shower of rain on a roof. "If you are a true seeker after knowledge, you need not fear."

"I, I guess I am," the boy said nervously as he peered over the stone rail of the bridge. Beneath him in the water was, as if reflected, the face of a beautiful woman, her long hair waving in the dark water, a kindly smile on her face. "Yes, I am the spirit of the river," she said, "and I am here to help you. Ask me what you will."

"Oh, um, that's very kind of you, ma'am," the boy stammered. "I, well, I seem to be having some trouble with my horse." He told her how he was supposed to plow his father's field but how the horse refused to cooperate, and he asked her to tell him the secret to making horses drink.

The spirit rose up out of the river to tower over the boy in a shimmering column of color and water, and perched on the stone wall beside him. Dripping cool water into his collar and down his back, *she leaned over him and whispered in his ear, "The secret to making horses drink is..."*

The boy leaned even closer to make sure he didn't miss anything.

"...the secret is..."

The boy waited eagerly.

"...you can't make a horse drink! Not if it doesn't want to."

The boy stepped back in surprise. "You can't make a horse drink? What sort of secret is that?" he cried out in disappointment. "I thought you were going to tell me how to solve my problem. Now you tell me I can't solve my problem at all."

The water spirit rested wetly on the balustrade of the bridge, her watery outline shimmering in the morning sunlight. She seemed to be laughing.

"What's so funny?" the boy asked in surprise. "Are you making fun of me?"

"No, no," the spirit said, still chuckling. "Although there is plenty I could make fun of if I were so inclined. No, that's not it at all. Like most humans, you assume there is some way you can force the horse to do what you want. But take a good look at your horse. It is ten times your size and twenty times as strong and it has been plowing fields since long before you were born."

"It has?" the boy said in surprise. "I didn't know it had been a farm horse before it came to us."

"You didn't know because you never asked it," the spirit said. "But I spoke to it yesterday, while you were running off to fetch your bucket. Your horse has done a great many things. It was once a champion racer too. It is far stronger and more experienced than you are. If it does not want to do something, what makes you think you can force it?"

"Okay, but if I can't force the horse to drink, then it won't be in shape to do the plowing, and then I can't get the fields prepared before the rains come. And then we won't have a good harvest, and then..."

"Yes, exactly," the river spirit agreed. "Then things will be dire indeed for you and your family. But does the horse care about those consequences? Does it even know?"

"The horse? Of course not, it's just a dumb animal. I have to do the thinking for it."

"Yes, and I'm just a dumb river, but here you are asking my advice," the spirit replied. *"Why don't you think about the gift I've given you and see if you can't come up with a solution to your problem?"* Then the spirit began to fade and flow back into the river below.

"What gift?" the boy cried. *"Wait a minute please!"*

"The secret," a far-away voice said from deep beneath the bridge. *"Your gift is the secret of making horses drink."*

The boy's thoughts were confused as he trudged the rest of the way to the field and harnessed the horse to the big plow once again. He was amazed to have seen and spoken with the river spirit, and glad that it had not done him any harm. On the other hand, he still had no idea what she had meant and was concerned he would not be able to get the work done on time.

His concern was justified when the horse once again got to the end of a row, stopped, and refused to turn and plow another furrow beside it. Try as he might, the boy could not get the horse to move. Even when some of the farmers from nearby fields came over to help, the horse refused to follow their lead. They all agreed it was the most stubborn horse they'd ever seen and advised him to trade it in for something more cooperative.

In desperation he left the horse there and ran all the way back to the bridge. Leaning over the railing, he called out to the river spirit and begged her to help him.

Her voice echoed up to him, saying, *"Did you figure out what to do?"*

"No, I'm sorry, but I didn't have any luck. I hitched the horse up and got it to plow one furrow, then it refused to do any more. One of the farmers told me I ought to trade it in for a run-down old nag and whip the nag to make it do what I want."

The river spirit's laughter echoed up from under the bridge. *"Then how much plowing would you get done?"* she asked. *"Could that old man's nag plow a field as big as the one you need to plant?"*

"I don't really think so," the boy admitted. *"It's just that I can't get anything done when this horse refuses to help. First it wouldn't drink,*

and now it won't even pull the plow. I want to take good care of it but I'm beginning to lose patience," the boy admitted.

"And why is it important to take good care of this horse?" the river spirit asked him, "since you say it won't do any work for you."

"My father always says we have to take good care of our horse because, 'Horses are our most important asset.' That's what he tells me."

"What do you think he means?" the spirit prompted.

"Well, I guess that since we can't do the work without them, we ought to put their needs first. That's why he wants me to make sure I take good care of the horse by feeding and watering it."

"Is that all there is to taking good care of a horse?" the river spirit asked him. "Do horses thrive on nothing but feed and water?"

"I, I guess so," the boy said. "What else could it possibly want?"

"Is food and water all you need in life?" the spirit asked him.

"Um, not really," the boy admitted. "I guess my family is important to me too. And I don't want to fail at this important job my father has given me. And I like to play with my friends from the village when I have time. And I've always wished I could go away to the city to study at the big school there but we don't have enough money. And..."

"You have many needs then?" she interrupted.

"Yes, but I'm not a horse."

"And so all the horse needs is its feed and water to be happy?"

The boy paused, puzzled, then he asked, "What do you mean 'to be happy?' Why does it matter how the horse feels? It's just supposed to pull the plow. I thought people kept horses so that the people could be happy."

The spirit smiled at him and said, "Perhaps that is what the people believe. But how happy can you be when your horse is unhappy?"

"What do you mean?" the boy said. "Is my horse unhappy?"

"It most certainly is," the spirit replied. "Haven't you noticed? It does not like the way you try to make it plow. It does not like the taste of the river water here, for the water is muddy from other horses wading into it. And your horse does not like being shut up in a little shed all the time. It wants to be able to graze through the meadows and gallop

and kick its heels up for fun. Oh no, your horse is not happy at all. It is not enjoying its new home."

"But if I let it run and play in the meadows," he said, "it might run away, and then what would my father say? Besides, how would I get it back when I needed it to do the plowing?"

"I don't know," the spirit said. "Why don't you ask the horse? Now off with you, I need to get back to my river."

"Wait! I don't know what you mean! How can I talk to my horse when it doesn't talk to me?"

"Of course it doesn't talk," the spirit said, laughing once again. "It's a horse, for goodness sake, not a person. But if you'll give it its head it will show you what it wants soon enough."

"Give it its head? You mean not lead it? Take the reins off of it?"

"Exactly. Why don't you try seeing where it leads you?"

The boy was much troubled by this advice for fear that the horse might run away. But he didn't know what else to do so he headed back toward the field with his mind made up to follow the horse instead of leading it.

As he drew near to his field again he was surprised to see a line of people. They seemed to be staring at something. Some of them were pointing and others were talking loudly and gesturing to each other. The boy hurried forward to see what the commotion was, fearful that something had happened to his horse.

What he saw was his horse trotting rapidly around the field, the plow cutting a deep furrow behind it. The horse's reins swung loose beneath its head. Despite the lack of a person to lead it the horse was working well. In fact, he didn't think he'd ever seen a horse plow as fast.

But the horse was not plowing neat furrows side by side, as was the custom. Instead, the horse was working from the outside of the field inward in a spiral pattern. It had already made a half-dozen spirals all around the field and it was looping around the next one at a rapid pace. The outermost one was square and followed the outside of the field, but with each loop inward the horse had rounded the corners just a little bit more, so that by now it was moving in a big looping line.

And as its course became less square and more rounded, the horse picked up speed.

Soon it was cantering along in a great oval, then galloping while the plow swished through the ground and kicked up a spray of dust and dirt behind it.

The horse looked for all the world like it was on a racetrack rather than a field. The boy realized with a grin that it was racing around the field as if it were on a track. The horse was making a race out of the plowing, and seemed to be enjoying every minute of it!

Soon the circles became too small for the horse to keep running and it slowed to a trot, spiraled gracefully to the very center of the field, and stopped.

The audience of farmers and field hands clapped and whistled, and some of them slapped the boy on his back and congratulated him. "That's quite a horse you've got there!" one of them said. "Never seen a horse plow a field that fast before. He made a real race of it, didn't he! Why, it would have taken me three days to plow that field with an ordinary horse, and here he's gone and done it in one morning."

"You sure got that horse well trained," another farmer told him. "Your father's going to be real pleased when he gets home."

The boy tried to explain that he hadn't had anything to do with it, then he walked out onto the field and stood beside the horse.

"I'm sorry I didn't listen to you," he told it. "You knew how you wanted to do the job all along, didn't you?" Then he patted the horse's shoulder and unhitched it from the plow. He reached up to grab the reins like he always did, then thought better of it and removed them too.

"Go ahead," he said. "Go wherever you want. I'll follow. I want to see what you're going to do next."

The horse looked at him for a moment, then it turned and trotted off the field, down the road, over the bridge and down the winding path to the watering place. The boy watched curiously from the top of the bank to see what would happen. The horse sniffed the water, then moved upstream a little ways and sniffed again. It repeated this behavior several times until it had moved a hundred feet or so away from the bridge to where a sandy beach marked a bend in the river. Here the horse finally seemed satisfied, and bent its head down for a long drink.

Then it searched the bank until it found a more direct way up, whereupon it climbed up onto the road. The boy scrambled after it and the two of them walked down the road side by side until they reached the cottage. Instead of going to its stall it walked to the back of the yard and began to nibble the grass in the shade of a large tree.

The boy left it there and went in to tell his grandmother what had happened. Just as he reached the house, his grandmother came running out and said, "Is it raining yet? I can feel it in my bones, it's going to rain today. You'd better get back out there, young man, and do some more plowing while you still can."

The boy looked at the sky and realized that big clouds were building on the far horizon. He smiled.

"Don't worry," he said, "the field is finished. There's just one thing about it though. It's not done in rows, it's done in a spiral. Do you think father will mind?"

His grandmother was pleased and surprised that he had finished the job so quickly, but she was not sure about the idea of a spiral pattern. "We've always planted and weeded and harvested in rows," she objected. "How will we do it now?"

"I'm not quite sure," the boy admitted, "but I have an idea that if we let the horse show us it will be easy. I have a feeling it knows what it's doing and will do a good job for us if we just let it have its head."

The father was skeptical too when he came home, and was at first angry with the boy. But it turned out the boy was right. At planting time they loaded the mechanical spreader with seed and harnessed it to the horse, then father and son stood and watched while it raced through the field in the same spiral pattern and sowed all the seed. The boy's father shook his head and said, "Who would have imagined! I seem to have *bought a race horse instead of a farm horse, but as long as it gets the job done this quickly I guess I don't mind."*

When it came time to pull the weeder through the fields, the horse retraced its spiral pattern again and quickly finished the job. And when it came time to harvest, the horse pulled a wagon the same way and the field hands and the boy and his father all worked behind it, racing to try to keep up. That year they had a bumper crop, and the boy was thankful indeed for the wisdom of the water spirit and the strength of the horse.

As they crossed the bridge for the last time that fall carrying home the final wagon load from their harvest, the boy paused for a moment to lean over the bridge and watch the water flow beneath it. His father asked him why he had stopped.

"Oh, I just wanted to say thank you to someone," he said. "This is where I first heard the secret of making horses drink."

"Secret? What secret?" the boy's father asked.

"That you can't make them drink," the boy said, laughing. "You can only let them drink. That's what I learned."

"Very good," the father said. "And nor can you make a boy be a farmer. I've been thinking. Are you sure you want to stay here and be a farmer like me, or is there something else you have a mind to do?"

The boy looked at his father in surprise. "Well, I sometimes think I'd like to go to school in the city," he said nervously. "Except of course we don't have the money for tuition, and you need me here to help with the farming."

The father smiled. "You're a great help, to be sure, but now that we have this horse I don't need you so very much. Why, he does most of the work without us! And as for money, if we are patient and frugal I am sure we can save enough eventually."

The boy felt like he was walking on air as they made their way home to the cottage. He hardly knew what he was doing as he rubbed the horse down and fetched a bucket of water for it from the well. "Wouldn't it be wonderful," he said to the horse as he put the bucket down in front of it, "if I could go to school this winter?"

The horse whinnied, then kicked the bucket of water all over the boy's feet.

"Hey! What'd you do that for!" the boy cried angrily. "I thought we had finished with that kind of thing." He stomped the water out of his boots angrily, then bent down to pick the bucket up and refill it.

Something shiny glittered from the pool of water beside the bucket.

The boy reached down and picked it up, then rubbed it on the fringe of his jacket.

It was a heavy gold coin, slightly dented, with a running horse on one side of it and a picture of a bridge over a river on the other.

In fact, the boy was certain it was the same coin he had lost in the river back in the spring. He had no idea how it could have gotten into his well, but there it was as real as could be, shining up from the palm of his hand. He wondered if the river spirit had been listening when he told his father of his wish to go to school. And he wondered what part the horse had played and whether it might somehow know a great deal more than he had realized.

The boy patted the horse on the neck, then ran into the cottage to tell his father he had found the money to pay for his tuition. He was so excited he could hardly contain himself. "At last," he thought, "my real education can begin." Of course the boy did not realize for many years to come that he had learned his most important lesson already, and that a stubborn horse is sometimes the best teacher of all.

C

The Discussion

When the woman had finished, the group of entrepreneurs and managers around her was silent for a moment, letting her story sink in. They had the feeling they had just listened to something that was more complex than its simple plot at first revealed.

"Well, what do you think?" she asked.

One of the older men in the group, who they had learned was the founder and chief executive of a successful firm, sat forward and said, "It's inspiring to me to see how the boy is finally able to succeed in his work and even to move on to new and better things. He achieves his successes not by doing good work himself, but by finally discovering how to make it possible for his *workhorse* to do great work. As managers and business owners ourselves, we need to recognize that our success is not directly in our own hands, it is in the hands of our employees. Their successes make it possible for us to succeed too."

"Yes," another person agreed, "it's amazing what you can accomplish when your entire organization is pulling together. But they don't always pull hard enough—or all in the same direction."

"Well, some workforces are better than others," someone else said. "What if all you've got is a scrawny old nag like that neighbor had instead of a strong, smart workhorse like the boy's?"

The older woman who had told them the story smiled and said, "But in real life, do you think that is how it works? Do you have to have a 'super' workforce to succeed? And if so, how is it possible for every one of us to hire above-average employees? Is that what the story really tells us?"

They thought for a minute, then one of them said, "I don't think that's the point. Remember that the boy at first thought he had a *bad* horse. It wasn't until he learned how to manage it well that he realized it was a great horse. It was the same horse, but his view of it changed."

"Too true," another put in. "I've noticed that when I'm focusing on the best qualities of my employees, things go a lot better and high performance is easier than when I'm focusing on the problems and feeling frustrated."

"That's a good point," a young manager agreed. "At first the boy saw his horse as a problem. That's how he treated it and that's the result he got. I wonder if you tend to get what you expect from your workforce?"

"Yes, especially if you think all they care about is doing the least work for the most amount of money," another person pointed out. "The boy did not understand the horse's needs, and I've heard that most managers do not know what really motivates their employees either."

"Another thing that reminded me of my work," a small business owner put in, "is when the boy was having a tug of war with the horse when he tried to force it to drink. The harder he pulled on the reins, the harder the horse pulled back. Sometimes my relationship with my employees gets a little like that and the story made me stop and ask myself who really wins when you get into a tug of war."

"Nobody does," the others agreed, and one of them added, "I think it is important that the horse started helping the boy only when the boy apologized and began to act more considerately toward it."

A woman who had been quiet so far spoke up and said, "I found myself wondering why the boy felt he had to control the horse's path when it was plowing. He was so sure he knew the one and only way to plow a field that he didn't even realize he was being controlling about it. Sometimes without really meaning to I don't permit my employees to be creative or to feel a real sense of pride in their own work. I think we often end up trying to control more aspects of the work than we need to. How does this make the employees feel?"

"When someone is overly controlling with me, it makes me irritated and I lose my enthusiasm," somebody said. "We have so much challenging work to do in my company that I don't think we can afford to waste *any* of our employees' natural enthusiasm."

"Good point," someone else agreed. "And did you notice that the boy trusted everybody else *except* his horse when he wanted to figure out what was wrong? One reason I think managers don't communicate as well as they could with their employees is that they often fail to realize that the employees are the leading experts on themselves. For instance, it is pretty rare for a manager to really stop and ask an employee what they want or need to do a better job or to be more motivated. Yet the employee is certainly going to have a useful perspective on that."

"Maybe it comes back to what we were saying earlier," another manager replied, "about how you get what you expect. If you see your employees one way, then you don't think to stop and ask them questions because you believe you already understand them."

"You are very good at finding insight in my story!" the older woman who had told it complimented them with a grin. "I'm impressed by all the ways you make it relevant to your work. What did you think about the coin the boy finds—does it have any special meaning for you?"

The group thought about it for a moment, then someone said, "I was interested in the part where the horse knocks the coin out of the boy's hand. To the boy it seems like the 'dumb horse' lost his coin by accident. But later on it seems like maybe the horse was trying to help the boy. Sometimes we may not realize it when our employees are trying to help us either."

"Yes," someone else added, "and all along the boy believes he is smarter than his horse. To relate that to our work as managers, what are the chances that any one of us is truly smarter than all our employees combined? That is, *if* we are able to tap into their full intelligence and knowledge. There are a lot of brains out there in my workforce, and maybe I don't put them to work as completely as I could."

The others nodded agreement, then one of them said, "I was struck by how the boy thought the coin was the treasure. I found myself asking what was the real treasure in this story and whether the boy would even know it when he found it. It turned out that wisdom was the treasure—the wisdom to take full advantage of his horse's potential."

"And that goes for our businesses too," they all agreed.

Then they saw that the next session of their seminar was starting and got up to go into the training room again. They were eager to see what practical tools and techniques they could pick up to help them apply the insights they had just gleaned from the story. And such is the power of story telling that each of them made a silent vow not to forget the "secret of making horses drink"—and to remember to pursue the wisdom needed to help people achieve their star potential more fully in their work.

(Based on *The Horse Who Wouldn't Drink*, copyright ©2001 Alex Hiam.)

BOOK 2

Horse Sense

Tips & Techniques for Managers

WHAT CAN WE LEARN ABOUT LEADERSHIP FROM THE ACTIONS AND
EXPERIENCES OF OTHER LEADERS?

1

Commitment

The bottom line is that a horse won't win any races it doesn't *want* to win. People work for their own reasons as well. Organizations succeed when their members want to succeed, not just because their managers want them to. The first task of any manager is to make sure the people are highly involved and committed.

> Make sure the horse wants to win the race too.

> *"I always thought the company wanted me to leave my brain at the gate."*
>
> —EMPLOYEE OF AN AUTO MANUFACTURER,
> AS QUOTED IN *THE LONDON TIMES*

"My job is cul-
ture cre-
ator, and I've
done my job if
salespeople leave
the sales meeting
feeling special,
like they're part of
the family."

—STEVE WRAY,
DIRECTOR OF SALES,
CHOLESTECH CORP.,
HAYWARD, CA
(SELLING POWER,
NOVEMBER/DECEMBER
2001, P. 73)

Traditionally, it might have been enough to be sure your people knew what was expected of them (or else). Today, we know we need employees who do far more than just show up. We need them to make sure everything is running smoothly, and to put their heads together to see if they can figure out a way to make the company even better. Companies need employees who are actively engaged in their work.

In my firm's leadership trainings, one of the things we do religiously is to ask participants to measure the level of commitment in their organization. Doing so achieves two goals. First, it clarifies whether this is an area that is worth their leadership effort—it usually is! Second, it helps clarify what exactly we mean by commitment. Here are some of the statements we use to describe commitment in that exercise (which we call POLO, short for *Profile of Leadership Opportunities*).

Would you say that employees

- care deeply about the success of their organization and its work?
- are doing productive work right now?
- are interested—their work does not bore them?
- feel a strong connection to their work group?
- feel personally responsible for at least some of the organization's results?
- are highly motivated by their work?

If you can give a hearty "yes" to each of these statements, then you have a wonderfully (and unusually) high level of employee commitment. What if your answer is a "sort of" or "not really?" That is not bad either, because it means that you have just identified a leadership domain that presents clear opportunities for your leadership efforts. Focus on building commitment and you can expect to see some solid results in your bottom-line measures of success.

How do you generate high commitment? There are a great many clever ways to tackle this challenge. In this chapter I'll share a collection of highly specific leadership actions and techniques because I always find that these are good sources of inspiration and translate more easily into action than more theoretical ideas do.

∪   ∪   ∪

Hiring Initiative

One good way to achieve high employee commitment is to look for commitment and motivation when you screen candidates. Yet companies usually seek people to fill positions based on qualifications—ensuring that candidates have the training and experience to do the job. If you think about it, this simply means we find people who can do the job well, but we don't really know if they will. (I like the distinction between can and will. Commitment is all about the will to do something—which if strong makes up for a lot of "can.")

When it comes time to evaluate qualified new employees after they are "in the saddle" we often find ourselves wishing they had a more gung ho attitude, that they took a little more initiative and tried harder. These are the intangibles that determine whether someone will achieve their full potential. Why not seek these intangibles in the hiring process rather than wish for them later on? That seems to be what motivates Jim Ansara, CEO of Shawmut Design and Construction (Boston, Massachusetts).

> "I don't think I'm the primary motivator. I give people license to be themselves and motivate others in that way. We give people the opportunity to be a maverick. You don't have to fit into a constraining mold at work—you can have a good time. We also try to show that what they do matters. That's why we share with employees the letters we get from passengers."
> —HERB KELLEHER, CHAIRMAN, SOUTHWEST AIRLINES (*THE WALL STREET JOURNAL* AUGUST 31, 1999, IN AN INTERVIEW WITH HAL LANCASTER)

"All the soft things that leaders have to focus on are becoming very important—areas such as professional and leadership development, work and family, and quality of life issues—whatever it is that gives your people a reason to be excited about waking up and going to work every day."

—KENNETH D. LEWIS, CEO, BANK OF AMERICA (*BUSINESSWEEK* DECEMBER 17, 2001, HEIDRICK & STRUGGLES SECTION)

Ansara describes what he looks for when interviewing job candidates.

I'm most impressed when someone has really dug into who we are and what we do. I'm turned off by someone who claims to have looked into our company, but has done very little preparation. There's no better clue that someone has no idea why they're here than when they tell us they're really interested in design. Our name is Shawmut Design and Construction, but we haven't done any design for over five years. (*San Francisco Chronicle*, December 30, 2001)

Ansara's approach could be adapted to many firms. Here are some thinking points to consider before *you* hire: What clues could you look for to find out how much initiative and effort a candidate has put into his or her approach to your firm? Does your current approach allow people to become serious candidates without having to try hard or demonstrate initiative? If so, could this be setting you up for commitment problems later on?

Find the "Actively Disengaged"

Here's an amazing fact: 20 percent of all employees (one in five!) are unclear on what they are expected to do, lack the materials to do their work, or are waiting for information from their boss. As a result they are actively disengaged, meaning they are not doing anything productive right now in their work. Oops.

A Gallup study revealed this unexpected problem and its most common causes. Now that we know many people are disengaged and waiting to be put back on track, the obvious leadership action is to keep a sharp eye out for this employee problem and when found, make sure these people get what they need to be productive again.

Here is a minichecklist of questions to help surface disengaged employees. Use it when you do a periodic walk-around. Ask yourself,

Does the employee:
- ❏ Know what is expected of them?
- ❏ Have the materials needed to do their job?
- ❏ Have anything important they should ask or tell their manager?

If you can't check all three boxes off for every employee, then you know you've got a problem. Now that it is visible, it shouldn't be so hard to fix.

Give Knowledge *and* Authority

Teams are formed frequently to improve quality and cut errors and costs from work processes. In fact, the improvement team is the most durable take-away of the quality movement and a majority of businesses use such teams. But often they get stuck. They run into a wall and can't seem to make productive changes. Conflicts arise, attendance slips, and employees want out. When this happened at a Whirlpool factory's dryer assembly unit, the team was turned around (with the help of consultants at R.V. Armstrong and Associates) by giving team members more authority to self-manage their work, plus giving them additional training in practical tools and techniques needed for process redesign.

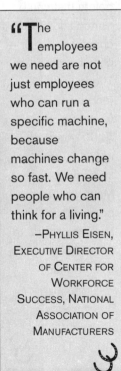

"The employees we need are not just employees who can run a specific machine, because machines change so fast. We need people who can think for a living."
–PHYLLIS EISEN, EXECUTIVE DIRECTOR OF CENTER FOR WORKFORCE SUCCESS, NATIONAL ASSOCIATION OF MANUFACTURERS

Mazda Motor of America replaced a cash incentive program for salespeople with one in which they call a special number each time they sell a car— and receive a randomly varying number of prize points that can be turned into merchandise of their choice later on. The rewards range in value from $25 to $250. According to Clark Colby, Incentives Manager, "The possibility of 'hitting it big' adds to the excitement of the program." (Program designed by BI Performance Services.)

The team went on to cut overhead, eliminate quality defects, and increase productivity by 70 percent. These sorts of results demonstrate the power of knowledge and authority combined. Self-managed teams without sufficient training exemplify the old adage, "Give them enough rope and they'll hang themselves." But when the authority to make decisions is combined with the knowledge to make *good* decisions, something magical happens and everybody wins.

Combating Boredom

What can you do to increase interest and encourage mental engagement with the work, especially if you sense that employees are falling into a boring routine or are finding their work dull and repetitive? This is a question we often address in leadership trainings my firm runs. Want to try your hand at it?

Imagine you have a group of employees who value excitement, and who sometimes feel their work is getting dull and repetitive. How might you use assignments, recognition, rewards, activities, or other treatments to pump things up and add some fun and excitement to their workplace? Come up with at least six ideas:

1._____
2._____
3._____
4._____
5._____
6._____

What did you come up with? Here are some ideas we've generated in past workshops. You could purchase

LEGAL PERSPECTIVE

Hiring—What Not to Ask

Whenever you interview possible new hires, prepare carefully so you know what not to say. Laws are very strict in this area. And while most rejected applicants do not take legal action, the occasional few do—and they can often find irregularities upon which to base a case.

Among the concerns you need to watch out for: Don't ask employees personal questions about their age, marital status, pregnancy, religion, national origin, race, sexual orientation, veteran status, health, and so forth. Any such questions may lead to claims of discrimination later on.

If a candidate tells you they missed a month of work last year, avoid the temptation to ask them if they were sick! From a legal perspective, you really don't want to know the answer to that question. (Indirect sources of information on health are also to be avoided, e.g., don't ask them if they have ever collected worker's compensation.)

Managers often assume they should not reject a candidate just because their attitude or personality does not fit the job or workplace. Actually, these can be legitimate concerns (but do document the reasons and relate them to requirements of the job). If you want to hire someone who is lively and self-motivated and shows a lot of initiative because these traits are necessary to perform the job well, then go ahead and seek someone with such qualities. But don't reject candidates based on age, gender, race, or other protected factors that ought not to have anything to do with ability to perform the job well.

A carefully prepared set of questions helps avoid such errors. Prepared questions also standardize the interview process, which is helpful in avoiding any appearance of inconsistent treatment.

—NANCY L. O'NEILL, ESQ. OF THE
NATIONAL EMPLOYMENT LAW FIRM JACKSON LEWIS

> "Employees feel good when they can use their knowledge and concern to help solve problems. The manner in which your company grants employees the authority to identify and correct problems reveals its level of commitment to participative management."
>
> —DICK MOORE, MANAGER OF TRAINING AND SAFETY, PLASTOMER CORP., LIVONIA, MICHIGAN (WRITING IN QUALITY DIGEST)

Do you conduct exit interviews? People who choose to leave your employment are a good source of ideas for how to make work more engaging. At software firm Cimnet Systems, exit interviews revealed that employees needed more feedback and wanted more opportunities to develop their skills. Employee retention and involvement improved when the company acted on these findings.

one of those relatively inexpensive coupon books (for restaurants, stores, movie theaters, etc.), then cut out a dozen of the best coupons and put them in a box or hat, and have a drawing in which each employee gets a coupon. Then you could have a bonus round drawing in which one of the employees wins an extra $50. This is a kind of crazy approach, but it is fun and can be an amusing highlight to the week. You could also ask two of your employees to make up a scavenger hunt, hiding clues and prizes for the others. Or how about starting a bulletin board where people post ideas for the most exciting weekend trip or craziest vacation—and then have a joke prize you give out to the employee whose entry is voted best? All of these ideas emphasize fun, adventure, and excitement and will help excitement-oriented employees keep up their enthusiasm.

Other strategies for combating boredom:

- Increase the level of challenge in their work.
- Tackle an exciting new growth goal.
- Ask individuals to suggest ways of redesigning their work processes to get better results.
- Form a quality improvement team.
- Offer job rotations.
- Try to finish the day's work an hour early for a special challenge—and then have a party in the extra time you saved.

Change for Change's Sake at General Electric

Have you ever heard of the "Hawthorne Effect"? At a GE plant in Hawthorne, New Jersey many years ago, researchers experimented with changes to the work environment to find out what might boost productivity. Surprisingly, they found that change itself seemed to have a significant effect. For instance, when they lowered the level of lighting, productivity went up for a while. Same when they raised it. If people are bored, almost any change may help them work!

Help Employees Develop Strong Ties with Each Other

Professor Peter Cappelli of the Wharton School and director of the Center for Human Resources argues that teamwork can help build employees' commitment to each other and thereby boost motivation and retention. In his words (from *Corporate University Review*) "It is easier for employees to feel a commitment to other individuals rather than an abstract entity such as the company."

Leaders like to think that people have a strong sense of loyalty to their employer but that is rarely the case today. Cappelli's suggestion to emphasize team loyalty is far more realistic. But how specifically might you use team affiliation to build employee commitment? Here are some suggestions that might help.

- Make sure every employee is an active participant in at least one team or group that interacts frequently.
- Keep an eye on how friendly those teams are and make it known that you are happy to move anyone to a new team if they aren't happy with their team. Some personality clashes are going to be far easier to avoid than fix. As a leader, you probably don't want to waste your time trying

> "Can you provide interesting work, or can you make the work that your people must do interesting in some way? There are many opportunities to do this if you think about it."
> —WILLIAM A. COHEN, *THE ART OF THE LEADER* (PRENTICE HALL PRESS, 2000)

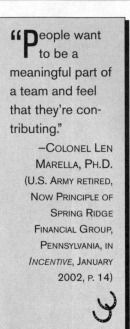

"**P**eople want to be a meaningful part of a team and feel that they're con-tributing."
—COLONEL LEN MARELLA, PH.D. (U.S. ARMY RETIRED, NOW PRINCIPLE OF SPRING RIDGE FINANCIAL GROUP, PENNSYLVANIA, IN *INCENTIVE*, JANUARY 2002, P. 14)

to make incompatible individuals like each other.

- Give employees plenty of opportunities to have fun or relax with their teams. If they only see each other under the pressure of task-specific meetings, they will probably not develop much of a rapport.
- Give the teams some interesting challenges to work on, not just routine boring stuff. (If you can't think of anything else, ask them to examine work processes and try to improve them to cut costs, avoid errors, or retain customers better.) A healthy challenge gives teams a purpose and their members a shared sense of accomplishment.

Remember, the teams aren't there just to get work done. They are also there to help employees develop a high level of personal involvement. Issues like motiva-tion, retention, and productivity are all about how employees *feel*, and their feelings toward work can be shaped to a large degree by their experiences as team members.

Why Not?

One company with polished floors in its hallways stages occasional Friday Olympics events in which employee teams do relay races in rolling office chairs (make sure there isn't a safety hazard!) and have con-tests for which team can make a paper airplane that flies farthest.

Giving Gifts

As a leader, one thing you can do to make your employees feel good and encourage them to take healthy responsibility for others is to help them organize a holiday gift-giving campaign. Individual employees can then go out and decide what they'd like to give, purchase and wrap it, and bring it to a central collection spot at their place of work. That's what Blue Cross Blue Shield of Illinois does each year, and the program collects approximately 2000 gifts which are then distributed to needy children in the community.

A Picture's Worth a Thousand Words

To give employees clear, up-to-date information on how things are going, create poster-sized graphs or charts in public spaces that track key measures of success like profits, sales, and quality indicators. If you don't have time to keep these charts up to date, ask employees to volunteer or rotate the responsibility. Also consider asking them what information they would like to have displayed so you can be sure they are getting the feedback they feel they need.

Let Employees Choose Their Bosses

The Madison, Wisconsin police department tried letting employees choose their bosses, and it seemed to work well. A decade ago they introduced a system in which officers are given the opportunity to choose their sergeants and sergeants can select the lieutenant they want to work under. So nobody has to feel "stuck" with a supervisor they don't get along with. Think about how wonderful it must feel to have control over who manages you on a daily basis and to know that if you are unhappy with your boss you can do something about it. That's a powerful lever to put in employees' hands and it is likely to make them feel

> "It is easier for employees to feel a commitment to other individuals rather than an abstract entity such as the company."
> —PETER CAPPELLI, WHARTON SCHOOL

> **Y**ou can raise employee involvement and foster a spirit of teamwork by inviting employees to give you feedback at the same time that you do their regularly scheduled performance review.

more in control of their fate in the workplace—and thus more committed, motivated, and optimistic in how they approach their work. I suspect it is one of the key reasons that the Madison police department gets exceptionally high satisfaction ratings from the people of that town, and also why jobs in this police department are always in high demand.

For Some Projects *Everyone* Needs to Be the Leader

How do you cut injuries in the workplace by a third in one year? Many manufacturers try to increase safety by using a combination of training and incentives (reward points that accrue over time for instance, or have managers who walk around handing out coupons to employees who are following correct safety procedures). But traditional programs are usually not as effective as an approach GM used throughout its North American facilities called the GM Safety Leadership Program.

What I find remarkable about this program is its message that *every* employee needs to be a leader when it comes to safety. Rather than bribing them to be more careful, it empowered them to recognize risky situations and behaviors and take action to prevent injuries. Each employee was trained in workplace safety and also in how to teach safety procedures to others. According to the company, "elimination of unsafe acts and correction of unsafe conditions is considered the responsibility of every employee."

I guess safety is too important to leave the leadership to a small cadre of managers. In fact, when you think about it there are probably many times when you'd like every employee to take a leadership role, not just in the pursuit of safety but in other important objectives as well. What would your business be like if you treated every employee like a leader? What would your management style be like? It's an interesting thought.

Supporting Kids and Young Artists in the Community

Blue Cross and Blue Shield of Illinois has a tradition of community involvement, and this has recently been extended to include purchasing works of art by Gallery 37 apprentice artists. (Gallery 37 is a non-profit group that showcases the artwork of Chicago's young people.) Other community projects include a Children's Garden of wildflowers, planted on a vacant block in Chicago. Projects like these are of great good for the community, but when you get the active involvement of employees, taking initiative to bring community projects to fruition, then they are remarkably good for the people in your company as well.

Let Employees Write Their Own News

In companies that have newsletters, the articles are often produced by someone nobody knows, and hidden away in a cubicle in the back of the Human Resources or Personnel Department. Management uses such publications as one-way communication vehicles and they don't do much heavy lifting when it comes to true leadership. A better idea is to have one column or page contributed by each department or function and let the employees decide what goes in and who does the writing. A truly open and participatory

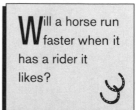

Will a horse run faster when it has a rider it likes?

How thirsty is
your horse?
• Does it want to
  win?
• Does it want to
  improve?
• Does it want to
  explore?
• Does it want to
  drink, or are
  you trying to
  force it?

organizational newsletter generates a lot more involvement and fosters more open communications. And it's a nice 'achievement high' for employees to see their own writing in print.

Ask Employees to Design Their Own Imprinted Merchandise

Companies purchase an immense amount of imprinted merchandise, from pens and mugs with the company name on them to T-shirts and other clothing, luggage, caps, and desk accessories. There is an eager industry awaiting your next order and able to supply customized merchandise at often remarkably moderate prices. But on the other hand, yet another product with the company logo on it may not be all that exciting to employees.

So here's a novel twist: Why not let each work group come up with a special tag line, motto, humorous cartoon, or logo of their own—and also choose what they want to imprint it on as a take-home reward? This could be a once-a-year project for employees, and you could even let them figure out how to coordinate the project and make a joint decision.

All you'd need to do is provide some catalogs and the phone numbers or Web addresses of a few of the larger suppliers and/or some local distributors. You'd also need to give them a budget (even if you can only spend $10 per person there are still plenty of options). If you don't have any knowledge of how to do this, send for a copy of *Incentive* magazine and read the ads in the back. Believe me, there are thousands of companies eager to fall over themselves to make you and your employees happy!

Replace Performance Reviews with Purpose Reviews

On the theory that employees work best when they see their work as relating to their own aspirations, Marjorie Miller of Miller Associates (a kitchen equipment wholesaler) replaced the annual performance review with a personal planning session for her employees in which they work on their own "life purpose" statements. The process includes a look back at your most satisfying experiences in life and then a look ahead at what you need to be doing based on what turns you on.

Ask Employees to Bring Learning Home

Debbie Reichenback of Tellabs says that "We challenge employees to take what they learn at work and use it at home. They meet weekly and share stories about how some technique or other worked out." For instance, maybe a minicourse on communicating better in conflicts helps improve communications with a spouse or teenage child. Or maybe someone uses new computer skills learned on the job to network home computers on a single high-speed Internet access line. Another employee took all the supervision and management courses he could, and applied the lessons to his volunteer work as a youth coach. There are many ways in which your people can benefit from what they learn at work. Encouraging people to take home their insights and expertise is a great way to make their work more relevant and meaningful. (See *Training*, May 2000, p. 65.)

Greening the Community

Agroup of employees from Atlanta-based power utility Jackson Electric Membership Corporation spent a day landscaping a new building for the Gwinnett Children's Shelter. Their work included seeding a lawn and planting ornamental trees.

Taking a Stand Against Cynicism

"**W**e live in a cynical society," believes Shawn Parr, CEO of San Diego public relations firm Bulldog Drummond. "We watch bad news on TV, roll our eyes, and then we click over and watch *Friends*. Well, this was different," he explained to *Entrepreneur* magazine, referring (as so many of us now do) to the terrible events of "9/11." Parr decided to put his firm to work raising money for the victims. Later on, other employees at the firm decided they wanted to maintain the effort and organized a 5K run/walk fundraiser. Although this is a relatively small firm, they raised close to 50 thousand dollars—and proved that they were a lot more committed and less cynical than they perhaps feared they were.

Ask Why a Task Is Important

Too often, employees find themselves working in the trenches, unable to see the links from what they are doing to broader benefits or purposes. Research shows that a clear "line of sight" from what employees do to *why* the work needs doing is a very powerful performance driver. Here are some examples of questions that help get an employee refocused on the distant reasons that give the current task meaning (from the *Motivational Leadership Workshop*, Alexander Hiam & Associates).

- Where does this go next?
- Why is it important to do this right now?
- What are the benefits of this?
- Just to make sure I understand the big picture, why exactly are you doing that? (Ask in a non-critical manner.)
- What impact does this work have on the customers?

Ask Instead of Tell

You often know what employees need to do, so it may feel natural to simply tell them. But to get them more engaged and build their self-sufficiency, it might be wiser to ask them instead. This technique is especially useful in any situation where you wish an employee would take more responsibility and initiative or gain skills instead of relying on yours. Try it next time someone comes to you for direction.

Here are some examples of helpful questions to guide them toward solving their own problem or making their own decision.

- What do you think the options are?
- How do you think you might handle this?
- Have you encountered similar problems before?
- What do you think the best starting point might be?
- What are the root causes?
- Why did this happen?
- What do you think you should do next?
- Have you run into similar situations in the past?

> **"I** can charge a man's battery, and then recharge it, and recharge it again. But it is only when he has his own generator that we can talk about motivation. He then needs no outside stimulation. He wants to do it."
>
> —FREDRICK HERZBERG

> "**V**igor is contagious, and whatever makes us think or feel strongly adds to our power and enlarges our field of action."
>
> —RALPH WALDO EMERSON

Questions like these may add a few minutes to an interaction with your employee, but I really believe they save you a lot of time later by helping the employee become more engaged in the work and a better self-manager.

The Power of Parties

Many workplaces use parties to bring people together for more social interactions than normal work allows. Leaders often assume a party is simply a treat or reward for good behavior, but in truth these gatherings are an excellent investment in raising employee involvement. They encourage people to make more personal connections with the group and the workplace, leading them to feel more of a sense of involvement and commitment to the work of the group. So gatherings and parties are probably most useful when things are going poorly and you need to raise involvement. Please don't wait for a success to hold a party—hold one now to increase the magnitude and frequency of future successes. (If you don't have a good excuse to party, then that is your excuse!)

Party Ideas

Here are some ideas in case you need inspiration: ice cream break; milk and cookie break; barbecue; take a group to lunch at a restaurant; order pizza, salads, and drinks and declare a lunch break; have birthday parties for employees; have birthday parties for employees' children; or have celebrations for any and all foreign holidays you can discover and order out for appropriate food. In other words, come up with many creative ways to celebrate and relax together and you will naturally generate high involvement.

Asking Employees to Organize Social Events

How about this for a fun twist on workplace parties? Give employees the challenge of putting on some sort of social event each week, and let them do the creative thinking and planning. (You might set time and expense limits in advance to give them some realistic parameters; you don't want to have to say no to their ideas after they are invested in them.)

Deferring to Employee Judgment

Hiroshi Yamauchi, President of Japanese game maker Nintendo, believes that the programmers working on a new product need to be satisfied with their work before it is released. Although deadlines are important and missing them is expensive, he considers development a delicate art and tries to listen to his employees rather than make top-down decisions about when something is ready. He was quoted as saying, "We always tell the developers to work on it until they feel it's finished."

Sometimes the employees really do know best, and part of the leader's wisdom is to know when to defer to them.

Parting Thoughts

I collect insightful quotes from all sorts of people, and often these seem to be a better source of inspiration than longer and more formal types of communication. Here are some of my favorites that I thought were particularly relevant to the challenges and benefits of raising employee commitment and getting them highly involved in their work and workplaces.

Only one out of every ten employees feels any obligation to stay with their current employer according to a recent survey by Walker Information and the Hudson Institute. What can you do as a business leader to improve upon this average?

*"No one keeps up his enthusiasm automatically.
Enthusiasm must be nourished with new actions, new
aspirations, new efforts, new vision."*

—PAPYRUS

*"Whatever course you have chosen for yourself
[and your employees], it will not be a chore but
an adventure if you bring to it a sense of the glory
of striving, if your sights are set far above the
merely secure and mediocre."*

—DAVID SARNOFF

*"Individuals have a need to feel successful in
their attempts to understand and master their
environment. This need for competence motivates
people to behave in ways that allow them to feel capable
and effective."*

—JAMES P. RAFFINI (UNIVERSITY OF
WISCONSIN-WHITEWATER)

The pursuit of employee commitment can be thought of from the employee's view as the pursuit of meaning and competence and involvement and many other good things that we all need in our lives and our work. Involving employees not only helps you achieve your goals better, it also helps *them* feel that they are doing meaningful work and that their contributions are valued.

Commitment Checklist

Here is a checklist highlighting tips and techniques for helping people feel more committed to their work and workplace.

✓ Seek new employees who demonstrate commitment and a high motivation to work for your company. They have the initiative to do the job—and that may be a better indicator of future performance than a long list of qualifications.

✓ Make sure every employee knows what to do and how to do it, and has the necessary materials and resources to get it done.

✓ Give employees plenty of opportunities and scope to solve problems.

✓ Make sure employees and teams have access to the knowledge needed to achieve their goals.

✓ Ask employees who quit to tell you what things bothered them most about the job.

✓ Make sure nobody is bored in their work.

✓ Encourage team members to build strong personal ties to their teammates and team.

✓ Encourage playfulness in the workplace. People who play well together work well together.

✓ Find ways to give employees a voice in choosing or at least evaluating their boss.

✓ Involve employees in charitable initiatives.

✓ Ferret out "Big Brother" policing of employees. Find ways to make employees more responsible for their own behavior.

✓ Ask employees to write a brief monthly newsletter for the company.

✓ Track progress against a major goal using publicly displayed visuals (a graph, pie chart, or thermometer) to share the data with everyone.

✓ Encourage employees to select logos and identities for their teams or projects and put them on personal merchandise of their choice.

✓ Ask thought-provoking questions and what-ifs as often as you can.

✓ Ask employees what they should do to solve a problem instead of telling them.

✓ Ask employees to design and put on social events and parties in the workplace.

✓ Make sure employees feel their work is completed to their satisfaction so they can take pride in it.

2

Communications

> Horse and rider
> must understand
> each other well
> enough to move
> as one.

A good rider is in constant, almost intuitive, touch with the horse. The horse and rider understand each other so well that they can act and think as one. Sometimes this means the "manager" is the one doing the listening, because often the horse knows best. It may know the way home or it might sense danger before its rider does. And it certainly knows when it is thirsty or hungry or needs a rest or wants a good hard run. The wise manager always listens to the horse.

> **D**oes someone have information *you* ought to see? Do you have information others ought to know?

"Look at this young lieutenant here. He seems to be paying attention. But he doesn't listen to what I say, he watches what I do."

—BRIGADIER GENERAL PAUL LEE, U.S. MARINE CORPS
(IN DAVID FREEDMAN'S *CORPS BUSINESS*)

I guess it is no surprise that great leaders are great communicators—or that organizations with high levels of achievement always seem to do a lot more and clearer communication than the average. After all, everything you do and say carries some message (something a good horseman knows too). When you ask employees what they value most and have the least of, they often say communication. Most employees do not seem to have a clear idea of what their leaders expect of them, nor do they have enough information about their work and workplace to satisfy their needs. Leaders who put creative effort and care into their own communications find it far easier to have a positive impact.

Even more, a healthy, vibrant work group has good communications in *all* directions. Each individual has ready access to the ideas and information of the others. Managing the communication flows and making sure they are healthy and accurate and rich in useful facts and inspirational ideas is an important calling for all leaders.

> **"I**n my opinion, a bad leader never gets bad news."
>
> –JIM SCOTT,
> CEO,
> THE CFO.COM
> (*SAN FRANCISCO CHRONICLE*
> JUNE 10, 2001, W7)

When we think about management communications, the first image that comes to mind is of a manager communicating: in other words, speaking or writing to others. But in reality, the most important part of a great leader's communication skills may be his or her ability to *listen*, not talk. I think of this as *leading by ear*.

Leaders who perfect the art of listening tend to ask lots of questions and seek many opinions first, before making a decision. They also know that simply listening to people is a powerful way to turn them on and get them involved. The act of listening is a demonstration of your belief in someone's capabilities. It tells them you think they are *important enough* to listen to.

Listening is a surprisingly powerful leadership tool, but it is also a relatively rare one. It seems that the higher someone is promoted, the harder of hearing they tend to become. You'd think that listening would be the easiest leadership skill, since all you have to do is open your ears and your mind to do it. But I've come to believe it is actually the hardest of the leadership arts.

I like to think of healthy communications as *rich* communications—rich in ideas and facts and opinions, and also in spirit and emotion and all the human elements of the striving for success. To create a rich communications environment, think about and try out some of the following ideas.

◡   ◡   ◡

Write Your Own Rumors

Rumors fly whenever employees are worried or a change is under way. Rumors usually exaggerate the problem and spread misinformation. Rumors are bad for morale and often lead to lower productivity and the defection of good employees. But not at Shaw's Supermarkets. During a tumultuous acquisition of another supermarket chain they started an in-house newsletter called *The Rumor Buster* in order

> **"N**umerous motivational studies show that employees typically place a high value on getting information about their job, their performance and how the company is doing."
>
> –BOB NELSON, AUTHOR, *1001 WAYS TO MOTIVATE EMPLOYEES* (WORKMAN PUBLISHING, 1994)

> In meetings, people talk mostly about knowledge they all share. That's a problem because something only one person knows about is unlikely to get discussed. Knowing this, you can make a special point of asking each person if they have any information that others in the meeting may not be aware of.

to make sure employees received accurate information. It is issued when necessary to share vital information and "bust" any inaccurate rumors that are circulating. Now the company's leaders get to write their own rumors, which means they can be sure the latest rumors are right.

Follow the 24-Hour Rule for Sharing Bad News

Howard Guttman, an executive coach, recommends asking your employees to tell you about any bad news or problems of any kind within 24 hours. Setting a time limit on negative feedback helps employees overcome their natural reluctance to pass bad news up the chain of command—and thereby increases the likelihood that the leader will actually find out what's going on.

Perhaps the best way to present the 24-hour rule is as a principle of good communication and something that the leader does too, so that everybody can trust everyone else to share bad news instead of hiding it. I wouldn't make it a top-down controlling thing that comes with negative consequences or you'll just add to the fear that keeps people from sharing bad news in the first place.

Model the behavior yourself by sharing any bad news you get that might be of interest to the people you manage. Then they'll see that you are serious about it and begin to do the same themselves.

Birthday Breakfast Meetings

This idea comes from Cisco Systems, whose President and CEO, John T. Chambers, holds a

LEGAL PERSPECTIVE

A Dearth of Documentation

It's an all too common scenario: A poor performer is given a number of undocumented corrections and warnings, until management finally loses patience and terminates the employee. Then the employee argues that he or she was discriminated against and was wrongfully terminated. To settle the claim, the company often has to pay a significant sum—*because in most cases there is no documentation* of the employee's poor performance. Whenever you are dealing with any performance problem or issue, make a note of it and make sure it gets into the employee's file. If the employee improves, you may never need that information, but if push comes to shove the documentation may save a lot of money and trouble.

—NANCY L. O'NEILL, ESQ. OF THE NATIONAL LABOR
AND EMPLOYMENT LAW FIRM JACKSON LEWIS

monthly "birthday breakfast." Invited: Every employee with a birthday in that month. They are encouraged to ask him anything they want—the tougher the questions the better. Chambers finds it an excellent source of candid feedback from his employees. But perhaps even more important is the fact of the invitation itself. Employees know they are invited and that their senior leader thinks them important enough to ask for their opinion—even if only once a year. In a company as big as Cisco, that is a good feeling for employees to have.

The Real Language of Leadership

The Jaguar company newsletter ran an article asking "What shadow do you cast? Being a good role

> **"S**traight from the horse's mouth" is an old expression meaning directly from the person or persons concerned—and that's still the best possible source for most information.

> "The employees ask tough questions, and by the time you've heard something a couple of times, you know that you've got a problem—or an opportunity."
>
> —JOHN CHAMBERS

model will encourage others to do the right thing (leading by example). Our children will always do what they SEE us do, and not what we TELL them to do." In fact, that probably goes for everyone, not just kids. The most effective leaders lead by example. Sometimes they don't even bother to put it in words.

The Stump-the-Leader Prize

AGI, an Illinois company, holds monthly meetings in which employees have a chance to question the CEO about anything they like. To make it clear that anything can be discussed, the employee who asks the toughest question is given a prize at the end of each meeting. I like this strategy and it reminds me of something I've tried in management trainings in which I bring a pile of good books and give one away whenever someone asks me a question I can't answer. It's a fun way to break down the barriers with your audience and signal that you are aware you are only human, and it encourages more active, intelligent involvement.

Recognize the Bear Necessities of Quality

For a fun way to recognize employees who come up with ways of improving quality, one leader started giving out a humorous award called the Koala T Award—which of course takes the form of a stuffed Koala Bear along with a certificate of appreciation. Humor adds a rich dimension to communications. Sometimes it pays to horse around a bit. (That is, as long as the joke isn't so bad that nobody can bear it.)

Put It in Stone

Would anybody remember the ten commandments if they had been communicated by e-mail?

To make sure employees remember an especially important message, hire a firm to etch it in stone and give each employee a copy of the stone message. Stoneworks Gallery of Tuxedo, New York, offers moderately priced etching into smooth, oval, palm-sized stones, and so do an increasing number of companies that take advantage of new laser cutting technologies. So leaders can now use stone to communicate a really important message. For instance, one small business owner and manager was facing new competition from a major chain that had opened in his town. He knew the only hope for survival was to cut costs and increase efficiencies, but his employees were used to the old ways and found it difficult to stay focused on the problem. By giving each of them a stone with the message, "Cut Costs Now" carved into it, he made sure his point was taken to heart. (He could have added "or we'll sink like a stone" if he wanted to really get their attention.)

Communicating a Vision

Vision, mission, purpose, direction, plan of action...call it what you will, it's still an important part of leadership. As a leader, you need to have an idea of where you want to lead your people. Then you need to communicate that idea clearly and well. But how?

Industrial psychologist Andrew DuBrin recommends "reinforcing" the message using lots of simple communication methods to communicate the mission or vision.

In companies where employees rate their managers as more concerned and considerate, employee motivation is highest and profits tend to be higher too according to studies by Chicago-based consulting and survey firm Surcon International. (Interesting question to ask yourself: *How considerate do I seem to my employees?*)

> **"The mere imparting of information is without education. Above all things, the effort must result in man thinking and doing for himself."**
>
> —CARTER G. WOODSON

As a consultant, I have often had opportunities to survey employees and ask them if they know what their organization's mission is. Most of the time they do not have the faintest idea. Sounds like a communication problem to me. So I think DuBrin's suggestions are a great idea. He recommends printing a short mission statement or description of your goal on plastic wallet-sized cards, small plaques that can be hung on key rings, or coffee mugs. To continue with this notion, why not use commonplace disposables like Post-it pads, note pads, and daily, weekly, or monthly calendars to communicate the message too? The more visible and consistent your message about the destination, the more likely your people will remember where they are supposed to be going.

Not Into Visions? Practical Plans Are Fine Too!

If you don't feel comfortable standing up and advocating for some exciting new vision of the future, that's okay. You don't always have to have a utopian future in mind to lead your people. A simple plan or strategy may be all you need. The key is that you ought to have *some* idea of where you want to go, and you need to share this idea with your people so they can help you get there.

For instance, a light manufacturer with mostly regional clients might not be ready for a grand vision like "Become a dominant global supplier." But a more practical plan like "Upgrade our process so we can get more out-of-state high-margin business" is nothing to sneeze at as far as leadership direction goes. The pursuit of high-margin out-of-state business can become your mission and you can focus on communicating it and engage your people in helping you figure out how to do it.

Any plan that seems likely to produce healthy growth is sufficient as a leadership vision and your people will appreciate having something to shoot for. In fact, the more practical and down to earth the vision, the more likely everybody will be to support it and make it real.

Peter Schutz told his people when he began the turnaround at Porsche that "we will never go to any race without the objective of winning." (He said it in reference to the company's plans for entering racing cars in Le Mans, the most important European car race, but he also meant it in the larger sense that he wanted the company to always strive to be the best at whatever it did.) They went on to win some major auto races and revitalize their company's image. But he didn't tell them they had to win any particular race—just that if they were going to enter one, they were going to try their best to win it. Small races are fine too if those are the ones you can realistically hope to win.

The Power of Present Tense Leadership

What is your business? What does it do? What is it best at? Sometimes simply *stating who you are* in a positive light is more effective than a vision of where you want to be in the future. When communicating a purpose or sense of direction, consider using the present tense instead of the future tense. Helping your people see your organization's strengths in a positive light can motivate them to use those strengths and build on them.

> One of the leader's key roles is to simply communicate a clear identity for the organization.

For instance, instead of a fancy mission statement about what your business wants to be when it grows up, you might simply say, "We are the best in our region at _____," or "We know how to make our customers happy," or "We deliver the best quality in the shortest time." These are examples of present-tense aspirational self-descriptions and they can be very powerful rallying calls for your employees. Unlike some future-tense vision, a present-tense description is clearly something everyone needs to live up to *right now*.

Write a "Recognition Note"

This is a remarkably simple but powerful leadership communication technique. The idea is to try to thank your people, praise them, or otherwise *let them know you are aware of their actions, effort, or accomplishment* by giving them informal, quick written feedback. Whenever an individual has done anything well or responded to a specific request or need, try to get them a quick written recognition note.

Keep your recognition notes very short and simple and use easy, informal media like sticky note pads, the backs of business cards, a selection from a box of assorted blank greeting cards, the bottom margin of a memo from the employee which you return with a recognition note, or of course e-mail.

Use Your Business Card for Appreciation Notes

The back of a business card has just enough room for a quick message like, "Thanks for your help with the research, I'll let you know how the project turns out," or "I appreciate all the hard work your department is doing, thanks!"

It is also a great place to scribble a quick thought-provoking question, like "How could we get in touch with lost customers to see what we did wrong?" Some business leaders use their cards for one-sentence motivational communications like these, leaving the cards on people's desks when they aren't around to receive the message in person.

See That Everyone Is Thanked

When the organization works hard toward a difficult goal, this collective effort needs to be recognized with thank-you's to everyone. Yet most often, leaders recognize the more prominent or higher-ranking contributors to the effort, or simply those who happen to be around and are easiest to thank.

To make sure everyone felt appreciated, one insurance company instituted a program they dubbed PEET, which stood for Program to Ensure that Everybody is Thanked. To implement it, managers spent a little time coming up with appropriate ways to thank people for their hard work and made sure they didn't overlook anyone.

Scripting Recognition Notes

Deciding to write something and actually writing it are two different things. I remember as a child my parents insisted that I write thank-you notes to distant relatives who had sent me presents. I'd stare at the blank sheet of paper for what seemed like hours, unable to figure out how to compose a natural-sounding thank-you to them. And in truth,

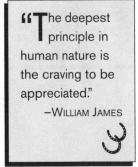

"The deepest principle in human nature is the craving to be appreciated."
—WILLIAM JAMES

So-called business cards are simply 2" by 3½" pieces of paper that happen to be easy to have made up at a print shop or even to print out on any desktop printer (try Avery's "Clean Edge No Perforations Business Cards" in sheets of ten). So why not make up Thank You note cards of your own? You can simply center the words *Thank You!* and if you like, add your own name in smaller print underneath.

most people still struggle with writer's block as adults, so it can be very helpful to have some examples and templates at hand when you want to write a recognition note. That way, you can quickly come up with some language that seems to fit the occasion and is different from the last time you wrote the employee. How much impact does the third note saying exactly the same thing have compared to the first one?

Here are some examples of simple but effective ways to scribble a recognition note.

- I appreciate your taking care of the _____ today.
- Thanks for doing _____. Good job. Well done!
- The _____ was helpful. Thanks.
- Got it, thanks.
- This looks good.
- Much appreciated.
- I see you finished _____. Great effort.
- Thanks for covering for me.
- That was very helpful.
- I noticed that you've been putting a lot of effort into the _____ lately. Thanks.

Using Probes

A probe is an exploratory question that checks or expands your understanding (and incidentally, often clarifies the other person's understanding too). Communications are often partial or inaccurate, so leaders can make extensive use of probes in all their conversations and in written communications as well. Warren Schmidt and B.J. Hateley (the authors of the famous book and training program *A Peacock in the Land of Penguins* and the new *Is It Always Right to be Right?*) teach managers to use probes such as

- Check your understanding by saying something like, "Let me check that I understand what you are saying. Are you saying that...?"
- Ask about motivations by saying something like, "Why do you want to...?" or "What makes you feel strongly about...?"
- Ask about issues and concerns by saying things like, "What do you feel is the most important issue?" and "Are there any other concerns you can think of?"
- Ask about goals or objectives, as in "What do you want to see come out of this?" or "What are you looking for?" or "What are your goals?"

Probes such as these can be used frequently to learn more about how people feel, what they care about, and what their concerns are.

Probing for Problems and Suggestions

You can also use probes to ask for suggestions and reveal problems that might need attention. Some business leaders stop and take the time to ask questions such as

- "Has anything gone wrong around here lately?"
- "Do you have any new ideas or suggestions today?"
- "Is there anything we could do to make this better?"
- "Do we have the right people working on this?"
- "Has anything surprising happened?"

Do you ask employees enough questions about their work?

- "Have any customers complained lately?"

If you don't ask—and ask with an appropriate probe—they probably won't say.

Coffee-Shop Meetings

One manager of a department for the city of San Francisco takes his staff out to a comfortable coffee shop for meetings. They pull some tables together, get the drinks and snacks of their choice, and settle in for a comfortable, relaxed meeting in which everyone is in a better frame of mind to listen to each other and be open minded.

Doing Something with Reports of Problems

When something goes wrong the leader ought to hear about it right away. As a leader you probably put some effort into trying to overcome employee resistance to giving the boss bad news (like making sure messengers know they won't be shot, right?). However, unless you clearly and visibly *do something* with the information, there is no reason why your employees should be motivated to report errors and problems. The trick is to make sure you and everyone around you has a productive action orientation toward errors and problems. The management at food producer Oscar Mayer uses a "claims analysis" strategy that exemplifies this point.

The key elements of their strategy are to

- make sure that all errors and problems are reported and recorded somewhere central so that there is a written database to look back on and learn from

- take immediate action, doing everything possible at the time the problem is detected to fix it and make the customer happy
- analyze the information about past problems to look for patterns and come up with ideas for prevention

When you embrace these three simple strategies, your employees will feel that reporting problems is a productive, helpful thing to do.

Try Asking Employees How to Lead Them

When IBM Corporation decided to increase the diversity of its hiring, managers targeted a variety of groups the company had relatively little experience with, such as disabled employees and seniors. To make sure leaders knew how to provide the best working environment for their new hires, they asked them a number of questions, including the following:

- What can we do to make you feel welcomed and valued here?
- What can we do to maximize your productivity?

Aren't those great questions? Odds are any manager would learn something new by asking any employee those two questions. Why don't you give it a try?

Ask Them What They Want
(Because You Don't Know Them as Well as You Think!)

Time after time, surveys in organizations reveal a fascinating disparity between what employees think about their work and what their leaders *think* they think. Managers often assume employees care most

> "As president of one of the largest soft drink franchises in the country, I'd go out in jeans and work as a driver's helper, a job I had in high school, to learn what our customers were thinking from our truck driver or 'route salesman,' as we'd call them in those days. At the end of the year, I'd switch jobs with the route salesman for a day and drive his route."
>
> —Vincent J. Naimoli, Managing General Partner/CEO, Tampa Bay Devil Rays and Chairman, President, and CEO, Anchor Industries International, Inc.

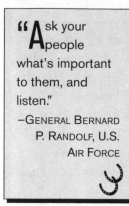

"Ask your people what's important to them, and listen."

—GENERAL BERNARD P. RANDOLF, U.S. AIR FORCE

about pay and other financially valuable rewards, along with promotions. But when asked, employees usually point to other factors as being more important to them. For instance, look at how far off managers were in guessing what employees' top workplace priorities are in a study done by professor Kenneth Kovach of George Mason University.

Employees' Top Three Priorities

1. Interesting work
2. Full appreciation for work done
3. Feeling included or "in on things"

What Managers Thought Employees Wanted

1. Good wages
2. Job security
3. Promotions and growth opportunities

In other words, they guessed wrong about the top three job needs of their people, which makes it unlikely that they'll satisfy those needs.

Let's Hear What Employees Think of Us

The idea of so-called 360 degree performance evaluations is not always popular with senior managers, who much prefer to evaluate rather than to be evaluated. But at software maker Lotus Development Corporation (an IBM subsidiary), employees told management that they thought employee morale would go up if they could provide feedback to their managers. Now even the top brass gets feedback from their employees and hears about it if they have any leadership failings the employees want to see fixed.

(Anonymous performance reviews work best to avoid the fear of retaliation from your boss.)

Before Signing/Sending Written Communications

Before you send any written communication, stop and ask this question about it: "What emotional message does it send?" We generally concentrate on the hard content—what to do, what you need to know, etc. That means the communications are functional in nature. When you stop and check the emotional message, you may find that your communication is more cool or impatient or critical than you really want to be. It is then an easy matter to add a few warmer words of support, recognition of hard work, or confidence in ability to handle upcoming challenges. Or just a friendly salutation to give your written communication a smile.

∪   ∪   ∪

Parting Thoughts

The *Financial Times* ran an interesting commentary by a top management consultant analyzing the United Kingdom version of the television program *Survivor*, in which she pointed out that it was an excellent case study of leadership in a fishbowl environment. In the show, she noted, both teams quickly voted out the two candidates who were the best qualified to help them win. The problem was that these leaders communicated poorly. They wanted to boss people around and came across as too directive and arrogant: "Nick Carter, a veteran of the Falklands war

> "If you want to gauge the health of an organization, tap into its grapevine, taste a sample or two, and test the toxicity. Companies that think they need to eradicate the rumor mill to clean up the culture have got it the wrong way around. Gossip is inevitable and blameless—the problem lies instead in its content, which reflects precisely what is going on in people's minds."
> —Nigel Nicholson, Ph.D., London Business School (in *Psychology Today*, June 2001, p. 41)

> **"We don't want to be led. We want to work as a team."**
> —FROM *SURVIVOR*

and a former Territorial Army leader, was voted out for being 'dictatorial' and 'a control freak.' Similarly, Jennifer Adams, a member of the opposing team and a former RAF corporal, was voted out in the next round. One team member said: 'She is far too over-powering for me. She's bossing people around. She's trying to lead everyone and we don't want to be led. We want to work as a team.'" (Quote from Michele Gorgodian, director of Integra Consulting.)

What if your employees could vote you out or in at the end of each week? Would it affect your communication style? In what ways? It certainly might cause you to listen a bit more than those two nonsurvivors described above.

When you think back to the story about the boy and the horse, what was his biggest mistake? Stories like that invite many different interpretations, but in my opinion the key issue was the boy's inability to really listen and communicate with his workhorse. The horse was communicating in its own way and signaling that it had motives, ideas, and needs, but the boy was not able to pick up on those signals. He needed divine intervention—something we aren't that likely to get in our work, so I guess we have to make do with any wisdom we can bring to stories like that and any ideas we can glean from inspiring examples such as we've seen in this chapter.

It all comes down to listening in the end. Or maybe the beginning. Maybe good management and great leadership *begins* with listening. The Chinese philosopher Lao Tzu said, "To lead the people, you must walk behind them." I bet he wanted you to do that so you could hear what they were saying and learn how they felt, don't you?

Leadership begins with listening to many things: To the "winds of change" and the broader economic environment so that you don't lead your people into the nearest brick wall. To the advice and experiences of those who've come before us in the hope that they have left us some good ideas and techniques we can use. To ourselves, so that we don't accidentally bring a negative attitude to work with us and "muddy the emotional waters" for everyone else.

And certainly leaders must communicate with their people, early and often. We need to listen for their ideas, we need to explore their needs, we need to use communications skills to inspire and focus and motivate them. And we certainly need to use listening to know when to use many other leadership skills.

You might not think communication has anything to do with riding horses, but all great riders are also great communicators—they are constantly in touch with their horse and are receptive to their horse's thoughts. Great communication is essential for leading horses, and for leading businesses well too.

Communications Checklist

Here is a checklist highlighting some of the best ideas and practices of the chapter.

- ✓ Respond to rumors with clear written statements of fact.
- ✓ Post graphics and charts to share performance data.
- ✓ Share bad news within 24 hours and ask everyone else to do so too.
- ✓ Hold Q&A sessions for all employees from time to time.

✓ Communicate by what you do and how you do it—actions speak louder than words.

✓ Write thank-you notes. Find ways to thank every one of your people.

✓ Let people know what your exciting vision of the future is (do you have one???).

✓ Talk often about your group's strengths.

✓ Check your understanding by probing to see what employees really mean.

✓ Find neutral, relaxed places like coffee shops to hold staff meetings.

✓ Encourage employees to share bad news with you.

✓ Shadow employees or try your hand at their jobs on occasion to make sure you understand their perspectives.

✓ Make a point of spending a little time with each employee each week so that natural opportunities for communication will arise.

✓ Find out what *really* motivates employees in their jobs.

3

Leader's Personal Perspective

I f the jockey is hesitant or uncertain the horse will also be hesitant and uncertain—and slower. Even though the jockey doesn't do the real work of running the race, his or her feelings and state of mind have a tremendous influence on the condition of the horse. The horse picks up on the rider's anxiety, fear or stress, and it knows when the rider is stressed—or happy. These feelings become its own.

> Tend to yourself. The horse knows how the rider is feeling.

> *"Employees want good mentors and leaders they can learn from."*
> —PAUL LEFORT, CIO, UNITED HEALTHGROUP

> **"** As we let our light shine, we unconsciously give other people the permission to do the same."
>
> —NELSON MANDELA

"Your behavior is the greatest influence over your subordinates in the work environment."

—FERDINAND F. FOURNIES (AUTHOR OF *COACHING FOR IMPROVED WORK PERFORMANCE*)

The first person every good manager must lead is him- or herself. How we feel about our work has a tremendous impact on our followers. In fact, some people believe that the special qualities of inspirational leaders flow from within and are a matter of attitude rather than anything specific about how they lead or what exactly they do.

Certainly your personal attitude has a great deal to do with how (and how well) you lead, and can affect your ability to use any of the techniques and strategies throughout this book. Look at it this way: How can you possibly expect to motivate your people and turn them on to a higher degree than *you* feel motivated and turned on yourself?

There is some wonderful new work in the area of "emotional intelligence" that shows just how powerfully contagious attitudes and feelings can be. For instance, in one experiment people are sent into a room to sit absolutely silent without interacting, in small groups, for just a few minutes. Then they all leave. Now, here is the interesting thing. The researchers evaluate each person's mood both before and after their brief exposure to each other. And they find that the brief time spent near strangers has a big impact on mood. What happens is that one person tends to spread their mood to all the others.

In riding, it's the rider whose mood affects the horse. In a business grouping or workplace, the person in the position of authority is typically the one whose mood spreads to the others.

So for starters, leaders need to make sure they are in the right frame of mind and feeling as motivated and positive about work as they want their people to be. That can be a tall order, which is why the self-management techniques in this section are so important.

Then there is the other little matter of how you get yourself *up* for the task of leadership each day. You must also decide how best to manage your time and effort so as to keep your leadership focused where it will do the most good.

To keep all your people up and focused and going in the right direction, you need to be up and focused and going in the right direction too. Your personal attitude toward leadership is yours to define—perhaps you even want to develop a personal leadership philosophy like some of the people in this section of the book have—but whatever your approach, it needs to be the foundation of your leadership. The ephemeral spirit of a turned on and fired up organization or work group stems all the way from the *personal* inspiration and approach of their leader. Leadership is a truly personal thing, even in the too-often-impersonal world of business. This section is devoted to helping you clarify your own perspective—a valuable exercise to do for at least a few moments each day before you climb back into the saddle.

Attitude is contagious. Am I *infecting* or *inoculating* my people today?

Do horses with happy, healthy, and motivated jockeys win more often than horses with depressed, stressed, or angry jockeys?

U   U   U

Employees Speak Out on Leadership

The following is from a nomination for Best Practices Award for Gerald Griffin, a manager with the National Weather Service. It was written by his employees.

Mr. Griffin has been our leader for a number of years. He goes above and beyond the call of duty to ensure that his team members are suitably recognized and rewarded for their accomplishments, yet his own contributions are generally overlooked. Team members who work for Mr. Griffin feel a high degree of loyalty and trust towards him because he places their interests and welfare above his own to ensure that they are treated fairly and with respect.

When a team member is overlooked or has a workplace concern he is ready to go to bat for them. He is fair to all employees under him, treats everyone the same, keeps his team informed of everything that is going on concerning work matters, and is very considerate of each individual. Always ready to lend an ear and help on personal problems. Open to any suggestions on improving team projects and always ready to help with problem tasks. He doesn't just sit back and assign a project to someone and forget about them. He works with them and does his share of the work too.

Communication, support, consideration, fairness—these are the qualities of leadership from the employee's perspective, and this organization has an interesting mechanism for letting employees talk about these qualities in a positive context. Each of the employee testimonials for nominees is posted for all to see—making it crystal clear what qualities employees value most in their leaders.

Keeping It Simple

Great leadership doesn't have to be a huge effort, since the goal is to let your people do what they do best. (That's *let*, not *make*.) As the leader, you aren't supposed to be doing the work. You're just supposed to make sure they do what they do well. That at least seems to have been the philosophy of Joe Torre, the legendary baseball coach who led the New York Yankees to a record number of wins and a World Series championship in 1998. Unlike many of the coaches whose teams he beat, Torre didn't jump up and down and shout at his players or rush onto the field to question every close call. He saw his job as "writing out a lineup card, making pitching changes, and patting guys on the back every once in a while."

According to one of his players, interviewed by the Associated Press during the World Series, "For the most part he lets us play." Not a bad strategy for leaders in general.

The Leadership Show Is Now Open!

"The office of Kay Fredricks—founder and Chairperson of TREND Enterprises, Inc., in New Brighton, Minnesota—is tastefully decorated and visible from the corridor that serves as the main passageway for employees to get to their workstations. Through large unobstructed windows,

> **"I**f you are not having fun in your job, there is something wrong."
>
> –Major General Albert B. Akers

> **"A** life is not important, except in the impact it has on other lives."
> —JACKIE ROBINSON

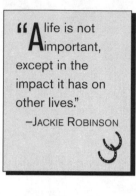

> **"N**o matter what I've faced, personally or professionally, what keeps me going is a passage from *The Life and Letters of Charles Darwin.* 'It's not the strongest or the smartest that survive, but the ones most adaptable to change.'"
> —DAVID STEWARD, CEO, WORLD WIDE TECHNOLOGY INC. (*BLACK ENTERPRISE,* NOVEMBER 2001, P. 80)

Fredricks can be observed in her office by anyone in the corridor. This open atmosphere is typical of Fredricks' management style and sets the standard for openness within the organization."

> —DONALD E. LEUSEY AND CHARLES LAVARONI, *THE EDUCATIONAL ENTREPRENEUR: MAKING A DIFFERENCE* (EDUPRENEUR PRESS, 2000, P. 79)

Know When to Change Your Style

"When I was running a division, my role was very different from running a corporation of our size and diversity. Along the way, I had to re-evaluate what leadership characteristics were needed for the job at hand. Few people recognize that when their job changes, their style should change as well. As a division president, for instance, you can be more direct and tactical; as a CEO, your role is more like that of a coach and a coordinator of other leaders."

> —STEVE REINEMUND, CEO, PEPSICO (*BUSINESS WEEK,* DECEMBER 17, 2001, HEIDRICK & STRUGGLES SECTION)

Unrelenting Pursuit of Quality

If I'd written this book ten years ago, it would have been full of quotes and examples from companies focusing on quality improvement. That was the inspiration of many successful leaders. But now quality is just another old fad, and few business leaders obsess about it any more.

However, if you are looking for a purpose or a new direction for your leadership, you might try revisiting this crumbling temple. While the quality religion may no longer be popular in executive circles, *quality still wins the day at ground level.*

The company that doesn't have to recall its product makes a lot more money than the one that does. And the company that provides a noticeably better service or product wins a higher share of sales and brings in greater returns on investment. Quality pays off if you pursue it hard enough to achieve quality that customers notice and get excited about. If you think there is any possibility of achieving noticeable improvements in quality, why not dedicate your leadership to this quest?

Obsess About the Details that Really Matter

Leaders delegate. They don't worry about details. Or so goes the conventional wisdom. In the hotel business, for example, CEOs have entire departments of peons to select carpets, sidetables, and bedsheets for rooms. Why would a CEO spend his days studying fabric swatches and paint samples? Because these details are the ones that really matter to the guest who wants to stay in a nice room, according to Barry Sternlicht, Chairman and CEO of Starwood Hotels and Resorts Worldwide, owners of Sheraton properties. "This stuff matters, especially if it's going to be replicated 10,000 times," he says, countering the criticisms of industry observers who accuse him of being too detail-oriented. Since the company has grown and prospered under his leadership, those so-called experts are beginning to wonder if they passed judgment too soon.

Truth is, while you don't want to worry about every detail, there are going to be some that really matter. Those are well worth a leader's time and attention. (Quote from *Business Week*, 11/20/2000, p. 142.)

> "Could Corporate America be deluding itself into thinking that quality no longer is the huge problem it once was?"
>
> –JEFFREY E. GARTEN, DEAN, YALE SCHOOL OF MANAGEMENT (*BUSINESS WEEK*, DECEMBER 18, 2000)

> You have to be able to look at yourself in the mirror every day and say, "I did the best I could."
>
> –BONNIE REITZ, SENIOR VICE PRESIDENT, CONTINENTAL AIRLINES (*FAST COMPANY*, DECEMBER 2001)

> **"We must reject not only stereotypes that others hold of us, but also the stereotypes we hold of ourselves."**
> —SHIRLEY CHISHOLM
>
> It is an interesting exercise for any leader to sit down and make a list of the self-stereotypes he or she holds. These are the imagined fences that keep you from going anywhere you want.

Be Your Customer

Goofy sports coaches in B movies are always telling their players to "be the ball." This is not very helpful advice in sports, but in business, it literally pays to be the customer. Or at least to take time to share your customers' experiences and stay in touch with the customer perspective on your business. A classic illustration of this point comes from the contrasting management styles of the executives of two great American hotel chains. Howard Johnson spent most of his time in his posh corporate headquarters in New York, allowing his once-dominant business to fall on bad times because he didn't realize his customers were no longer happy with his prices and service. In comparison, Marriott used to visit hundreds of his chain's hotels each year and he expected his managers to do the same. He had a much clearer idea of what his business looked like from the customer's point of view…and the business prospered as a result.

Customer Care Day at Xerox

Xerox executives don't lose touch with customer concerns because one of them is in charge of dealing with complaints each day. The idea is that leaders can easily fall out of touch with the "front lines" of customer service unless they spend a little time out there. To solve this problem, Xerox instituted Customer Care Day for its 40 most senior managers. Each takes a turn as duty officer for the day and is responsible for listening to any customer complaints that come into headquarters. Listening and *resolving* complaints, I should say. At first it was nasty duty since the phone tended to ring off the hook. But the experience spurred managers to lead an aggressive effort to improve the quality of products and services, and the number of calls gradually fell. Nothing like direct customer feedback to let you know what needs improving…whether you lead a small business or a multinational.

Eyes of the Beholder

When we ask business leaders about their behavior, they often describe themselves differently from how their employees describe them. For instance, there is usually a big difference in views of how good they are as listeners, whether they keep their people fully informed, and whether they praise good performance or not.

Are leaders unusually blind when evaluating their own behavior? No, in fact many business leaders may have a *more* realistic view of themselves than people typically do, since self-awareness is an important element of leadership success. In general, people have a surprisingly poor ability to see themselves as others do, and people usually describe their own interpersonal behavior far more favorably than others do.

This general self-bias was illustrated beautifully by a recent ORC International survey asking people about manners. In it, 85 percent of respondents rate their *own* manners as good or excellent—but if they are correct in this self-evaluation, then how come only 23 percent of them rate *others'* manners as good or excellent? That's a pretty big gap. Either most people have great manners, or more than three fourths of all people have poor manners. Which is it?

What matters in manners—as in any interpersonal behaviors—is how they are *seen*, not how they are

> "If what you are doing doesn't work, stop doing it."
> —FERDINAND F. FOURNIES, *COACHING FOR IMPROVED WORK PERFORMANCE*

This advice may sound obvious but is surprisingly hard to put into practice! Try making a list of things you keep doing even though they don't get the desired results. Then come up with a new response for each of those situations.

"**W**hen I was an impressionable account executive, each of my bosses taught me at least one nugget that I use with my team now."

—RICHARD LEWIS,
WORLDWIDE
ACCOUNT DIRECTOR,
ABSOLUT VODKA,
TBWA/CHIAT/DAY
(*NEW YORK TIMES*,
JANUARY 5, 2002)

Interesting exercise: Try making a list of "nuggets" learned from each of your past bosses. Then think of ways to *use them.*

intended. What this survey tells us is that most people, most of the time, are not being nearly as polite and well mannered as they think they are.

Applying this to leadership, what if leaders are wrong about their own behavior even half as often as the average person is? They will still seem rude or irritated or unthankful or not interested in listening when they mean to appear quite the opposite.

It is a strong reminder that good leadership requires unusual attention to and interest in one's own behavior. The leader who can accurately judge the impression he or she makes is a long way ahead of the average person—who thinks they are being polite while others see them as rude.

LEGAL PERSPECTIVE

Caring Too Much

Being considerate and polite is good management, and helps prevent conflicts with and legal actions by employees too. However, being too personal can have quite the opposite effect, leading to claims of harassment and other legal hassles. The distinction is subtle. For instance, a manager might notice that an employee has begun to act tired and distracted and is performing below par. Wanting to be considerate, the manager might ask the employee if everything is okay at home or if s/he is feeling down or depressed for some reason. These personal questions might reveal something that puts the employee in a protected class (for instance, depression can be considered a disability under federal and state laws, and you can't discriminate on the basis of a disability). Even more surprising to many managers, the employee might believe the manager thinks s/he is depressed—and this could be interpreted as the manager regarding the employee as disabled due to depression, even if the employee does not actually suffer from depression. Either way, if the employee is later terminated for poor performance, the manager's personal questions may be used against him or her by the employee who may claim he or she was fired because the manager regarded him/her as disabled.

Try to focus your questions on the specific work behavior of concern, and avoid asking personal questions about what might have caused it. You can show consideration by offering to help the employee improve their work, rather than by asking about their personal life.

Similarly, employees must not be discriminated against (treated differently or worse) because of their age, gender, health, religion, marital status, race, national origin and so on. A single mother struggling to raise young children might well deserve some consideration from her managers, but it is still wise to avoid asking her personal questions about how things are going at home. You don't want her to feel you are singling her out.

–NANCY L. O'NEILL, ESQ. OF THE NATIONAL LABOR
AND EMPLOYMENT LAW FIRM JACKSON LEWIS

Key Qualities of Marine Corps Leaders

The U.S. Marine Corps selects its leaders through a trial-by-fire process. Candidates spend ten weeks undergoing rigorous screening at the Office Candidate School in Quantico, Virginia. There are many tests of academic and physical skills, and these contribute to whether candidates make the grade or not. But the most important single factor is their leadership ability, and it is often evaluated in the field by instructors with clipboards who observe each candidate as he or she struggles to lead a group of fellow candidates through a difficult trial (see sidebar for an

> **"A** group is trying desperately to lever a barrel over a large wood pyramid with poles. One candidate slips and drops his pole, which hits a red zone. 'Boom!' yells the instructor. The leader looks stricken, and for several moments the group stands there, miserable. It's this loss of momentum, of course, rather than the dropped pole, that counts against the leader."
>
> —DAVID H. FREEDMAN, *CORPS BUSINESS: THE 30 MANAGEMENT PRINCIPLES OF THE U.S. MARINES* (HARPERBUSINESS, 2000, P. 141)

example. Some leaders fail to organize or motivate their groups. Others try to do everything themselves or take excessive risks and get "killed." A few make it through the grueling tests by demonstrating consistently good leadership.

Seven weeks of constant testing may seem like a pretty lengthy job interview compared to the screening given managers in the business sector. But in truth, it is barely enough to really see how they perform under the pressures of leadership situations. There is a lot to be learned by how officer candidates fail at Quantico. Here are some of the most common errors.

- Not taking initiative to organize or help others
- Failing to ask for input from the others in the group
- Sticking to a plan too long after you should have seen that it was failing
- Failing to build rapport with others—so they don't support you when you need them to
- Not listening well; making up your mind before hearing all the information
- Taking excessive risks or burdens on yourself; trying to do it all

(List based on reporting by David Freedman in *Corps Business.*)

In Officer Candidate School, such leadership gaffs can get you thrown out. The Marine Corps is very cautious about who it trusts to lead its people. But in business, leaders often go on for years without even realizing they are making these common errors.

Resetting

Resetting is putting the past behind you and starting fresh, even if things didn't work out as well as you hoped last time. Rapid resetting is a key skill in successful leadership. Here is an insight into how to reset quickly, using a key word to remind you of this important skill.

> *"If a prospect says no, go to the next one on your list. If an idea doesn't work, immediately go to the next one. 'Next' is the most important word I know. Whenever something doesn't work for me, I just tell myself, 'Next!' It works."*
>
> —MARK VICTOR HANSEN, COCREATOR OF *CHICKEN SOUP FOR THE SOUL* (INTERVIEWED IN *SELLING POWER* MAGAZINE)

Winning the "Head Game"

Here are some interesting thoughts to keep in mind as you prepare yourself for another day of leadership:

> *"It is not as much a matter of tennis as it is of mental fitness."*
>
> —JUAN CARLOS FERRERO, AFTER LOSING A FRENCH OPEN SEMIFINAL MATCH, JUNE 2001

> *"What is the most important play in soccer? The most important play in soccer is the next play."*
>
> —BORA MILUTINOVIC (WORLD CUP SOCCER COACH)

> *"Success or failure in business is caused more by mental attitude even than by mental capacities."*
>
> —WALTER DILL SCOTT (EXECUTIVE)

> "I know from past experience how challenging it can be to stabilize a company and to motivate employees during a time of dramatic cost-cutting and difficult decisions. But I am optimistic."
>
> –JACK CREIGHTON, CEO, UNITED AIRLINES

> **"L**ife has two rules:
> Number one, never quit;
> number two, always remember rule number one.
>
> –DUKE ELLINGTON, MUSICIAN

The Courage to Cry

"The deeper that sorrow carves into your being, the more joy you can contain."

—KHALIL GIBRAN

Maybe one of the hardest lessons of leadership is knowing when to feel sorrow. Sometimes things truly *are* bad, in which case the leader may not only be excused for feeling sorry, but may even *need* to feel sorrow as a way of getting in touch with the situation and preparing to lead the way out of it. It can take considerable courage to allow yourself to cry. As leaders, we are sometimes called upon to feel others' pain more fully than we might wish.

I was truly struck by the frank admission of Sima Samar, minister of women's affairs in post-Taliban Afghanistan, that she spent the first three days of her new administration crying. The stories of suffering during five years of Taliban rule that she and her staff were hearing were simply overwhelming. As quoted by the Associated Press (December 30, 2001), she explained that "Women were really traumatized so much that we just started crying. We didn't know what else to do."

But that was just for the first three days. Then they got to work. Samar's first step was to adopt a more free and fearless approach to administration. She proudly explained to the press that "I am the only minister who doesn't have a gunman standing outside."

Positive Persistence

In my firm's leadership workshops we often teach a principle called positive persistence. It is the common theme running through almost every entrepreneurial success, technical breakthrough, or turnaround of a failing business. What is it?

It is a combination of optimism, determination, and creative problem solving. Persistence alone is not enough, because after all, banging your head against a wall is persistent. But it is not effective. A positive belief in the possibility of solutions leads you to examine that wall carefully and find a way over, around, under, or through it. Or you might find a way to blow it up or simply avoid it and go somewhere else. Great leaders always exhibit positive persistence and spread this powerful attitude to their people. To simplify only slightly, all you really have to do to be a great leader is to make a vow to yourself that you will approach challenges with a higher-than-average level of positive persistence! (My book *Doing the Impossible* explores this in more detail.)

How Do You See Yourself?

Remember the advice of Helen Keller, perhaps the greatest contemporary example of a person who focused on her own strengths rather than weaknesses as she overcame her extreme disabilities. She said,

> *One can never consent to creep when one feels*
> *an impulse to soar.*

Do You Have a Credo?

Some business leaders define their philosophy and write it down to remind themselves of how they want to lead. Here's an interesting example.

- Ready. Fire! Aim.
- If it ain't broke ... break it!
- Hire crazies.

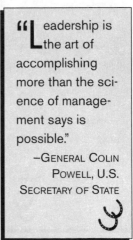

"Leadership is the art of accomplishing more than the science of management says is possible."

–GENERAL COLIN POWELL, U.S. SECRETARY OF STATE

- Ask dumb questions.
- Pursue failure.
- Lead, follow ... or get out of the way!
- Spread confusion.
- Ditch your office.
- Read odd stuff.
- Avoid moderation!

—THE LEADERSHIP CREDO OF KEVIN ROBERTS,
CEO, SAATCHI & SAATCHI WORLDWIDE

Do *You* Have a Leadership Philosophy?

I'm always impressed to meet a leader who has defined his or her approach to leadership and is able to communicate it effectively. It's helpful for the leader to be clear on these things, and it sure makes things easier when the followers know what their leader believes in. Here's a good example of someone who is able to articulate a clear philosophy with ease.

My philosophy can be summed up in three short words: "Do What's Right!" Let me explain what I mean. I consider six elements crucial to "Do What's Right!" These are: Integrity, Loyalty, Teamwork, Individual Initiative, Communications, and Taking Care of Our People.

These elements are all closely interwoven and are mutually supporting. They are inseparable and that's the way I treat them.

—MAJOR GENERAL ALBERT B. AKERS

One of the activities my firm uses in leadership workshops and retreats is to give each participant a sheet of paper with a big star on it. Their task is to label each point of the star with one of the key components of their own personal leadership philosophy: what they believe it takes to be a star and help the organization be one too. It's a challenging exercise but it helps clarify one's personal leadership philosophy. Why not give it a try?

Leading from Values

Personal values are an important part of a leadership philosophy, and without them leaders sometimes wander into trouble. With them, however, a leader's path is often made clearer, as in this case:

> When an employee from a competitor offered to sell him a valuable customer database for $20,000, Andrew Parsons, vice president for sales and marketing at Vector Networks, promptly reported the attempt to the chief executive of the competing company, NetSupport.
>
> (*THE WALL STREET JOURNAL*, JANUARY 28, 2002, P. C4)

Later, Parsons received a call from the FBI and agreed to participate in a "sting" operation that caught the criminal in the act of handing over data for cash.

Being "Real" at Marconi

Marconi, a British IT and communications company, embraced a set of values to help it grow that included one of the more intriguing goals I've heard of for a company. They want everyone to be "real people" which they define like this: "Marconi people are straight talkers, people who say what they mean and mean what they say."

"Contrary to what we usually believe, the best moments in our lives are not the passive, receptive, relaxing times—although such experiences can also be enjoyable, if we have worked hard to attain them. The best moments usually occur when a person's body or mind is stretched to its limits in a voluntary effort to accomplish something difficult and worthwhile."

—MIHALY CSIKZENTMIHALYI IN *FLOW: THE PSYCHOLOGY OF OPTIMAL EXPERIENCE* (HARPERCOLLINS, 1991)

In leadership trainings that my firm puts on, we call this quality genuineness, and have found in our surveys that it is highly prized by employees—but remarkably rare in their leaders. The idea is to stop hiding who you are and how you feel behind a corporate mask and start relating on a more real and honest level. When you do, it does wonders for communications, builds trust, and increases your people's commitment to a surprising degree.

Your Brain: Use It or Lose It

I find it fascinating to see that, of the many executives I get to meet in my work, the ones who have the most actively curious minds are often the ones who seem most successful and resilient in their careers too. Perhaps John Zenger puts his finger on the reason for this when he observes that

> *"There is strong evidence that people who exercise their brains improve their ability to think and solve problems. They also prevent or postpone mental deterioration as they age. Turning off a mindless television program to read a book or even do a crossword puzzle may preserve your brain."*
>
> —JOHN H. ZENGER, CHAIRMAN, TIMES MIRROR GROUP

Release Your Own Stress to Lead More Calmly

Pity the leaders in any organization. They are ultimately responsible for anything that goes wrong. They are the ones who have to worry about what to do next or resolve conflicts and problems within their organization. Leadership is, let's face it, a highly stressful endeavor. Yet good leadership requires calmness and an ability to rise above the daily stresses and stay cool and collected.

Great leaders are still smiling when all hell breaks loose, and their ability to avoid stress inoculates their entire organization against this enemy from within. So how can leaders (like you) be less affected by stress and lead your people by example? How can you feel more calm and collected than those around you so that you can provide emotional leadership and keep everyone positive and productive, even in the face of chaos and confusion?

Well, one thing's for sure. It won't happen just because you want it to. Some people are naturally more calm than others, but everyone responds to stressful events in basically the same way: they get stressed! So to get rid of your own stress (and lead the way to eliminating it in others), you need to adopt some practices that zap stress and keep it from taking control of you. Here are some simple things you can do while you work.

- Tense up your fists for a few seconds, then gradually relax them to let the stress flow out of your muscles. If it feels good but doesn't completely eliminate your tension, try this tense-then-release pattern in other muscles (your arms, neck and shoulders, feet, buttocks, stomach, etc.). Breathe deeply to enhance the effect of this exercise.
- Take a humor break. Keep a book of jokes or cartoons at hand and stop for a minute to look through it when you need to release the tension. As soon as you find yourself laughing naturally over a good joke, you will discover you've defused the tension and can go back to work with a new, healthier feeling.

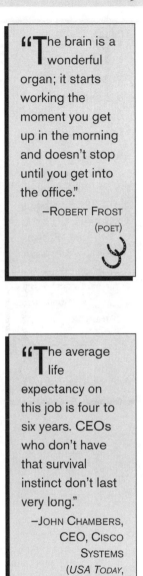

"The brain is a wonderful organ; it starts working the moment you get up in the morning and doesn't stop until you get into the office."
—ROBERT FROST
(POET)

"The average life expectancy on this job is four to six years. CEOs who don't have that survival instinct don't last very long."
—JOHN CHAMBERS,
CEO, CISCO
SYSTEMS
(USA TODAY,
DECEMBER 31, 2001,
P. 1B)

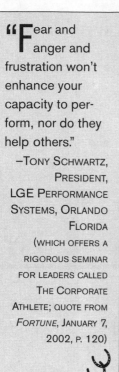

"Fear and anger and frustration won't enhance your capacity to perform, nor do they help others."
—TONY SCHWARTZ, PRESIDENT, LGE PERFORMANCE SYSTEMS, ORLANDO FLORIDA (WHICH OFFERS A RIGOROUS SEMINAR FOR LEADERS CALLED THE CORPORATE ATHLETE; QUOTE FROM FORTUNE, JANUARY 7, 2002, P. 120)

- Make a "minichange" to improve your workplace or working life. According to Robert Epstein, author of *The Big Book of Stress Relief Games*, "Small changes have BIG outcomes," at least when you make them yourself and they eliminate any of those all-too-common sources of minor irritation. For instance, the telephone on my desk rings so loudly that it startles me and interrupts my chain of thought. After ten interruptions, I'm getting irritable and stressed without even realizing it. Could I make a minichange that eliminates this problem? Sure—now that I'm thinking about it. In fact, I just turned the ringer down to low after writing that sentence. Funny I hadn't ever examined the phone carefully enough to notice there was a control on it before!

- Breathe deeply and calmly ten times. Yes, ten whole times; don't cheat and stop early. If you doubt the power of this technique, do it right away before reading another sentence. There, see what I mean? (By the way, have you ever wondered why cigarette breaks are relaxing? It's largely because smoking a cigarette forces the smoker to take a series of slow, deep breaths. I'm not suggesting smoking, but why not take a breathing break? Step outside the nearest door and breathe deeply ten times. You'll feel better, guaranteed.)

- Make a list of things that make you feel good at work. Keep it at hand (i.e., post it inside the top drawer of your desk) for quick reference when you need it. Next time you start feeling stressed or irritable, check the list and make yourself pick an activity from it to do right away. For instance, my list includes "call my kids" and "walk around the block" and "make a cup of tea."

Humility as a Leadership Technique

PeopleSoft, Inc. CEO David Duffield earned a reputation as a sincere and accessible leader by moving his office into a cubicle just like the ones his employees use.

Bill Belichick, Super Bowl-winning coach of the New England Patriots, received a complaint on a road trip that one of his top players had been given a small, uncomfortable hotel room instead of the suite he thought he deserved. It must have been tempting to tell him to stop being a baby, but instead, the coach decided to teach a lesson in humility by example— and switched rooms with him.

Providing Emotional Leadership

It's hard to keep the mood in your workplace up and positive unless you feel that way yourself, so one of the activities we do with managers in our leadership trainings is to have them brainstorm ways of making themselves feel good when they are having one of those low moments at work. Here are the instructions we give them. See if you can do this activity on your own—then keep your list on hand for reference when you next need it.

ACTIVITY

Identify Actions that make you *Feel Better*

Goal: Come up with a list of at least five things you can do to help yourself feel better.

Feel better = improve your mood, boost your physical or emotional well-being.

> I don't know why every organization doesn't have a humor bookshelf. It is the cheapest and most effective remedy for stress in the world.

> The wise leader knows that managing his or her own stress is the surest way to reduce stress *throughout the organization.*

> **"W**ork with your values. They last, and so will you."
>
> —IIDA AND JAY FROST, FOUNDERS, THOUSAND CRANES TEA, FAIRFIELD, CONNECTICUT

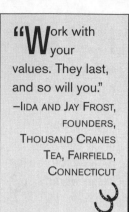

Constraints: Each action should take no more than a few minutes to complete. Each action should be suitable to your workplace.

This one is for you to fill in on your own. Good luck, I know you can do it!

1. _____

2. _____

3. _____

4. _____

5. _____

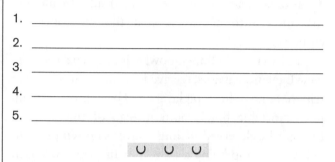

Parting Thoughts

I just spent an afternoon at a TEC group meeting. TEC stands for The Executive Council, and they have been organizing local circles of business executives since the year I was born, 1957. The executives meet once a month to share ideas and problems, offer each other suggestions, and learn together—they often bring in a speaker for example.

I'm telling you this because spending time with business owners and top executives always reminds me of what a high-stress job they have. This group was certainly no exception. Some of them were concerned about the economic downturn and its impact on their businesses and whether they might have to lay people off. One told the story of how he had to fire his CEO and come back from retirement himself to save his business. But what struck me about the group most was how much fun they had and how easily they relaxed and were able to support each other in that forum. They could really let their hair down and talk about things with fellow executives that they could probably never do back at the office. And they gave each other a lot of emotional support as well as helpful advice. This monthly meeting was, for them, a way of taking care of their own personal perspectives. It helped them gain insight, relax, and return to their work with renewed enthusiasm and a sense of humor.

Every leader needs such activities because every leader needs to manage his or her own personal perspective before managing the business. Remember the lesson experienced riders tell us, that the horse can tell how the rider feels? In fact, if you've ever been around horses, you know they can pick up your feelings the moment you enter the stall. They can tell by your touch as you saddle them how you are doing. You don't need to be in the saddle to share those feelings with a horse; in fact it probably knows more about your personal perspective than you do. So if you neglect yourself, you are simply going to externalize any problems and find they have gotten a lot bigger and harder to deal with than if you had handled them when they were yours alone. The only thing I like less than being stressed out myself is having to handle a stressed-out horse!

Here are a few more parting thoughts, these perhaps a bit more profound since I stole them all from others.

"There are two things over which you have complete dominion, authority, and control—your mind and your mouth."

—MOLEFI KETE ASANTE

Perpetual optimism is a force multiplier.

—GENERAL COLIN POWELL, U.S. SECRETARY OF STATE
AND CHAIRMAN (RET.), JOINT CHIEFS OF STAFF

"GE Medical Systems lost out on a multi-million-dollar deal to provide diagnostic equipment to a big hospital. The sales staff sadly accepted the loss; Jeffrey R. Immelt, the chief executive, refused to." Immelt re-mobilized his troops went on to close the apparently impossible deal. As *The New York Times* puts it, "Colleagues, college friends—and, decisively, Mr. Welch—paint Mr. Immelt as a man whose vocabulary does not include the phrase 'It can't be done.'"

–*THE NEW YORK TIMES*, DECEMBER 1, 2000, P. C1

"Take your work seriously, and yourself lightly."

—THE MOTTO OF PLAYFAIR, A CONSULTANCY THAT
SPECIALIZES IN BRINGING FUN TO THE WORKPLACE

*"If you want to manage somebody, manage yourself.
Do that well and you'll be ready to stop managing. And
start leading."*

—UNITED TECHNOLOGIES CORPORATION'S
INSTRUCTIONS TO NEW MANAGERS

*"Far away in the sunshine are my highest aspirations.
I may not reach them, but I can look up and see
their beauty, believe in them and try to follow
where they lead."*

—LOUISA MAY ALCOTT (WRITER)

Personal Perspective Checklist

Here is a quick checklist highlighting some of the best ideas and practices from this chapter.

- ✓ Check your own attitude before trying to work on anyone else's!

- ✓ Recognize the qualities in yourself that employees value most (how fair, considerate, and supportive you are).

- ✓ Stay calm and "let them play."

- ✓ Stop worrying about your employees and start taking care of yourself if you find your work is no longer fun.

- ✓ *Trust people* in order to bring out the best in them.

- ✓ Realize that your people work hard and try hard much of the time, and be thankful for it.

- ✓ *Do* sweat the details that matter most to your employees or customers.

✓ Focus more on doing the right things than on doing things right.

✓ Take charge of maintaining the momentum.

✓ Be prepared to abandon any plan that appears to be failing.

✓ Focus on strengths—your own and others.

✓ Be as real, honest, and genuine as you can possibly be. Be yourself.

✓ Read, solve puzzles, ask questions—exercise your brain.

✓ Develop practices that reduce your stress. Be a calm leader, not a stressed one.

✓ Be as optimistic as you possibly can. If you can't, then stop briefly to do something that makes you feel better.

4

Supervision

> You have to ride the horse, you can't just sit there.

Riding is an active endeavor requiring constant adjustments on the part of the rider. There are many styles of riding, but all of them involve ongoing, active effort by the rider as well as the horse. The fastest riders are highly skilled and active in their approach. The same is true of managers. To keep your organization moving, you've got to take an active approach to moving along with it. You don't take the steps, but you do have to be there guiding and challenging it every step of the way.

"My view is what keeps people at a place and motivated is a sense of direction, of purpose."
—HENRY SCHACHT, CEO, LUCENT TECHNOLOGIES INC.
(*BUSINESS WEEK*, MAY 7, 2001, P. 106)

The work itself is what employees interact with and live with constantly. It is what they do, what they get paid for, what their job *is*. That work can be motivating, exciting, challenging, a great learning experience, a wonderful stepping stone to advancement—or it can be a drag, a bore, stressful, dull, dangerous, stupid, meaningless, without purpose, a rat race, a treadmill. In short, the work itself can have a huge influence on the people who do it, just as they have a huge influence on the work. Get the people matched with the right challenges and they blossom, and the bottom line grows too.

If people are not properly challenged with work they like, find meaningful, and are motivated to do, then there is very little you can do as a leader to fix the situation. That continuous relationship between the employee and their work is too pervasive and powerful for any leader to overcome with good leadership. In fact, good leadership is wasted on bad work.

That is why the best leaders always keep an eye on the work itself, and view structuring and supervising employee tasks as a key part of their leadership role. They make sure everyone has a good "line of sight" from what they are doing to some darn good reason for why it needs to be done. They make sure everyone has the resources and skills needed to tackle their challenges with just the right amount of stretch— enough to excite them but not so much as to scare them or produce unhealthy levels of stress. What exactly do these effective leaders do to make sure the work is supervised well with an eye to producing inspired performances?

Good leadership is wasted on poorly designed work.

Give Employees Checklists for Producing Great Results

Usually managers focus attention on desired results by penalizing those who fall short and recognizing or rewarding those who achieve them. But results are the outcome of specific behaviors, so it is often better to focus on the behaviors instead. Make up a list of the three to six most important things to do (keep it positive—a don't list is not as likely to engage employee attention). For instance, for employees who take customer orders over the phone, the list might include:

- Check your understanding by repeating the information back to them
- Ask if there is anything else you can help them with
- Smile and thank them for their order
- Remember to process the order right away

If you, the leader, believe that these behaviors are likely to produce happy customers and to avoid confusion, delays, and errors, then giving employees this checklist and encouraging them to use it is a powerful way to get good results.

Encourage Employees to Design/Improve Their Performance Checklists

To engage employees more fully, encourage them to propose changes or additions to their performance checklists. Or even better, instead of writing the description of how to do a good job yourself, facilitate a discussion among employees who do the work and guide them as they produce their own checklist. Let them design and produce it in the form they find most useful too. (Preprinted notepad? Poster on wall? Wallet reminder card?) Get them involved and it will be more useful and a lot more likely to be used!

Motivate by Sharing Specific Gains, Not General Profits

Many companies have experimented with employee profit-sharing plans, and in principle they should work well since they align the employees' financial interests with the company's. The problem is that individual employees feel pretty far removed from the bottom line of the income statement and don't see

> If you value my work, then show me by giving me valuable work to do.

clearly enough how what they do affects the results. If profitability seems out of their direct control, it will lack motivating power.

But studies of gainsharing plans indicate that they can work far better. What they do is link a reward (or even simple recognition) to one specific and measurable goal that is more directly in the employees' control. For instance, in one supermarket chain employees in some of the stores were offered bonuses if the stores' payroll costs were kept at or below 9.5 percent of sales.

Now, employees felt they could control this number by watching things like excessive "sick" days and overtime that make labor costs get out of control, or by helping to boost sales through friendly service, good selection, and display of merchandise. This was a game they could win. Sales went up by a quarter in the stores using this gainsharing plan and labor costs fell, even taking the bonuses into account.

The Best Recognition Is a Good New Assignment

Most managers say the trick to motivating employees is to give them recognition and rewards—and so they offer cash bonuses, certificates of appreciation, and other pats on the back. But when you ask employees, they often see it differently. To them, the best recognition of their worth is to be selected for a challenging, important new assignment or task. Their attitude often seems to be, "If you value my work, then show me by giving me valuable work to do." Select good employees for an important or highly visible job or role and you give them powerful evidence that they are truly appreciated. (If you haven't got any plum assignments to give out, then get creative and come up with some projects that your good performers can do. No point wasting all that talent!)

Don't Force People to Do Bad Work

Motivation expert Dean Spitzer points out that employees *want* to do a good job. Pride in a job well done is one of the most powerful motivators. But too often, we design or manage the work so as to make it impossible to do an excellent job. This sets up a basic disconnect for employees that leads to frustration and early burnout. For instance, if you insist that employees handle customer calls quickly, you may be forcing them to brush off complaints instead of resolving them properly. (I'm convinced that red-tape barriers to doing a good job are a *major* cause of poor attitudes and resignation letters. This is a good issue for any leader to work on.)

Devote a Day to Good Works

Deloitte Consulting staged an annual IMPACT Day in which many employees work on community projects and do volunteer work for charities. By saving this date on the calendar, the leaders ensure that employees take the idea of community work seriously and they encourage people to put some of their work time and other resources into the effort. I am sure that many employees are active in their communities throughout the year, but much of their effort is outside of work. The special day dedicated to such efforts helps make them more visible and shows that the company supports its employees in their charitable endeavors.

> "I appreciate the respect I receive for a job well done. That does not necessarily equate to more money, but it feels good to have someone request my presence on a team or as part of an effort."
>
> —AN EMPLOYEE RESPONDING TO A SURVEY ON RECOGNITION BY TONI LAMOTTA (FROM *RECOGNITION THE QUALITY WAY,* QUALITY RESOURCES, 1995, P. 148)

LEGAL PERSPECTIVE

Fundraising and Bulletin Boards

Many employers may wish to maintain some control over what is solicited and posted in the workplace (for instance, if employers are not currently unionized, managers may not like the idea of outsiders being able to solicit employees during working time because it can be disruptive). Yet if you permit many other organizations to solicit or post information in the workplace, you can't expect to keep ones you don't like out. Employers cannot enforce no-solicitation rules aimed at limiting union solicitation if there are too many exceptions. There isn't much difference between a company-sponsored fundraising event, charity drive, or solicitations from employees to sell products like makeup, and a union membership drive, so limit the number of employer-sponsored charities and prohibit all other types of solicitation if you want to maintain control over access to your employees during working hours and in work areas.

—Nancy L. O'Neill, Esq. of the national labor
and employment law firm Jackson Lewis

Recognize Conservation Initiatives

Many employees work in "mature" work processes that they don't have a lot of opportunities to change or improve. That can be dull, and bored employees are employees without the challenges and opportunities that turn people on and bring out high levels of motivation and commitment. Challenging employees to find ways to make a business more earth-friendly is a great way to end-run this problem. Anything they come up with is likely to benefit the company directly too, since usually conservation and waste-reduction saves the company money as well as helping the environment.

Bell Atlantic uses this strategy to good effect, and also offers an Environmental Excellence Award to an employee or team each Earth Day to help spread the word within the company. For example, one team of employees came up with the bright idea of changing the cooling system for the air compressors needed in the company's central offices. I don't know quite what air compressors do in maintaining cable service, but apparently they are important and the company used to use millions of gallons of water each year to keep them cool. Now, due to some hard thinking by employees, the compressors run on a new "closed loop" cooling system that recycles antifreeze and avoids all that wasted water.

This is good thinking, and a great example of employees taking initiative instead of just punching the clock. The more opportunities like this you can give your employees, the better.

You Can't Afford Not to Pay Them Well

Steve Balmner, Microsoft's CEO, is big on cutting costs, but when it comes to the payroll, he is a contrarian. In fact, when he took over the top job from Bill Gates, he immediately set about raising salaries in order to ensure that Microsoft's 40,000 employees were paid better than people in equivalent jobs at 65 percent of competing companies. The idea is to make sure that nobody you value feels they are undervalued.

On the Other Hand...
Don't Expect Pay to Do the Motivating
In one major study, employees reported they wanted on average 25 percent more pay than they now get—regardless of what their current pay rate is or how

Challenges are great motivators—when employees see them as opportunities rather than problems.

> The thirsty horse won't work hard, but on the other hand, a horse that has had too much water won't work at all.

recently they received a raise. Nobody thinks they are overpaid. And even if they did think they were overpaid, it wouldn't lead most people to work any harder than they do now. (If you doubled everyone's pay today, would they produce twice as much tomorrow? I doubt it. In fact, productivity might actually go down.)

Just make sure your people are not underpaid, since pay is far more powerful as a demotivator than a motivator.

Providing a Healthy Level of Challenge

Psychologists have known for a long time that people need the right level of challenge to function well and be self-motivated. Too much challenge is debilitating and produces anxiety and stress. Too little is boring and can also lead to a feeling of entitlement and a lack of initiative. But give someone a job that requires them to stretch a little and you'll often see peak performances.

Now new research adds urgency to this principle of good on-the-job leadership by showing that people who have either too much or too little challenge in their work are at high risk of substance abuse. Greg Oldham of the University of Illinois at Urbana-Champaign and his associates found higher levels of smoking, drinking, and use of illegal drugs among employees who found their work either too simple or too challenging. The work literally drove them to drink, or worse.

Their conclusions? "People may use substances to soothe the frustration they experience as a result of being over- or under-stretched by their jobs." (*Journal of Health and Social Behavior*) They recommend that managers regularly measure an employee's strengths and weaknesses and match them to appropriately rewarding work. In other words, manage the assignments you give your people, and the amount of support and assistance for doing those assignments, based on what an appropriate level of challenge is. You want them to feel that their work is an exciting and rewarding stretch. If you aren't sure you've got the mix right, you can always try asking them.

How to Challenge Complacent Performers

Sometimes the leader has to give an employee a wake-up call. You don't want to play tough all the time of course. But it is essential to challenge employees when they do not recognize that there are significant problems requiring them to change their ways and they insist on pretending it's business as usual. So how do you deliver the wake-up call?

First, timing is important, as illustrated by George Karl, coach of the Milwaukee Bucks basketball team. He watched his players throw away what should have been an easy game against the Washington Wizards...their fourth loss in a row in November of 2001. It was obvious to everyone except the team's star players that there were major problems they needed to fix, and the team's under-performance in that game brought the problem to a head. (Lesson #1: Use a particular instance of under-performance or other visible crisis to set the stage for your wake-up call.)

Next, Coach Karl called each of his key "star players" into his office and delivered his criticism and challenged them to play more as a team. The lesson here?

> Stars radiate light. Black holes absorb energy. We need to invest in our stars—not our black holes!

Make sure you come through loud and clear, and make it obvious that you are NOT treating this like business as usual. They need to sense that this is a turning point for you and for them. Coach Karl later told reporters that he really laid it on the line, even calling his players irresponsible "millionaire crybabies" at one point. He also repeated his criticism and concerns in public and to the media to make it clear he would not back down until they responded appropriately. (Lesson #2: Make it absolutely clear that you see this as a crisis that demands immediate change on the part of employees so they can't ignore your concerns.)

Finally, Coach Karl did not accept or even listen to his players' views. Usually a good leader needs to be a good listener, but as Karl sensed, when it comes time to challenge them you need to play a more directive, assertive role. Later on, when interviewed about those player meetings, he would tell reporters he couldn't even remember what his players said—except that some of their language was colorful—because he wasn't interested in what they had to say at that point. (Lesson #3: If the time has come to challenge your employees, recognize that your style has to be strong and assertive and that the communication should be one way.)

In training leaders in how to use multiple styles depending on the situation at hand, I often cover what we call the *challenge* style of leadership. It's not for everyday use. But when complacency or overconfidence are blinding your people to the grim realities of the situation, then considerate management has to be put on hold while you work on getting them in touch with reality. When that's the priority, I recommend following the lead of this professional basketball coach. Heck, it worked for him. His team had a hang-dog 3 to 9 record when he issued his challenge. Afterward the record turned around and the team won 49 of its remaining games and lost only 21. Sometimes a wake-up call is truly the best medicine, and it falls to the leader to prescribe and deliver it. But be careful not to use this style too often or your people won't take you seriously.

Lesson #4 from Coach Karl is found in the fact that he only used that challenge style once, at the moment in his team's season where he felt it would do the most good. And that helped mark the moment as a turning point each one of his players would remember and point to at the end of the successful season.

Don't Set the Bar Too High

Challenges are motivating. We have a natural desire to climb mountains, cross rivers, and solve mysteries. Yet give someone a challenge that is too difficult and they will lose motivation and probably fail. Which means *you* fail in your efforts to lead them. That's what happened at Chase Bank according to one employee who quit a good sales job there because the sales goals seemed impossible. Although he was outselling many of his associates, he still felt badly about his work. Then as he was leaving his manager admitted that he had been told to set the goals so high that fewer than 40 percent of salespeople could achieve them. The manager didn't want to lose him, but the damage had already been done.

The lesson? Avoid the temptation to set ever-higher goals. Goals alone don't produce great performances. It takes a positive attitude too, so if goals

To issue a wake-up call,

1. focus on a specific situation.
2. define it as a crisis.
3. be strong and clear.
4. don't do it too often (or they'll think you are "the leader who cried wolf").

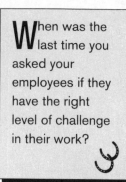

When was the last time you asked your employees if they have the right level of challenge in their work?

are unrealistic they will discourage instead of encourage.

Check the level of challenge by *talking to each employee* about their current goals and how challenging those goals feel to them.

- *Tell them* you want to give them good stretch goals that have some degree of difficulty, but are not impossible to achieve.
- *Ask them* if they have the right goals to feel excited about their work. Adjust goals together with them if necessary.

Most leaders never stop to discuss the level of challenge with their people, and yet people respond very positively to any efforts to make sure the challenge is appropriate.

Stay Focused on Each Employee's Key Assignment

Everyone is busy in the workplace, but what exactly are they busy *doing*? As a leader, you want to know that each of your people is focused on something important. A great way to do that is to decide what each employee's most important assignment is, and then reinforce the importance of that assignment by asking them how it is going on a regular basis.

One manager does it this way. She maintains a list on a white board in her office of all the things each person is working on. Then she permits herself to *underline in red just one of those assignments* for each employee. The underlined task is the one she thinks is most important, and she is careful to mention and monitor that task every day. Otherwise, her attention is naturally drawn to the newest projects and to any jobs that are going wrong, which means she may unconsciously be focusing on the wrong things and not talking to her people about their most important activities.

There is a lot of interest in *how* leaders interact with their people and whether they are providing the kind of inspiration and support needed. This method gets at something far simpler and more fundamental: *what* you talk about. This can be an incredibly powerful leadership tool. For instance, the manager who says service needs to improve, and then actually remembers to ask each employee about their contributions to service improvement every day, is going to get some significant progress just by virtue of ensuring a constant focus on the goal.

Assign Improvement Goals

Most managers give their employees a list of things to do. A powerful lesson from the many companies that have implemented quality management is that people are more inspired when their leader asks them to do something *better*. You don't need a formal quality program or any special tools or training to harness the power of this simple leadership technique.

Just pick one thing for each employee or group/team of employees that you think they could improve upon (choose something they have enough control over to make it possible for them to improve it). Ask them to think about how to do the work better. Suggest that they find some simple way to measure the quality of the work (like number produced, speed of turnaround, percentage of leads converted to customers, etc.). Then ask them to see if they can find ways to improve.

To train a horse to jump a high fence you start out with a low fence and work your way up gradually. Organizations need to be trained in the same manner.

Check back in with them periodically and you will generally be rewarded by an enthusiastic description of how they are doing. But don't be critical if there is no improvement. The real benefit of this approach is that it gets your people involved in *trying* to improve, so make sure you recognize and praise effort as well as results.

Bring Meaning to Assembly-Line Jobs

Antonio, Texas-based USAA has millions of customers for its property and casualty insurance, so you can imagine how many insurance applications the company must process. Like most insurance companies, USAA used to handle applications in an assembly-line fashion, passing them from one desk and department to another until all the steps were completed. No longer. CEO Robert McDermott redesigned the process so individual employees handle individual applications and customers, taking more responsibility and having more control over their work and the customer's experience. The drive to make the work more meaningful for employees has paid off in happier customers and growing revenues, and it has also helped cut employee turnover and increase employee loyalty. USAA's competitors lose 42 percent of their call-center employees a year on average, but USAA only loses 6 percent, which means USAA saves a lot on recruiting and training costs and has happier and more experienced employees on the front lines to talk to its customers. (*Bloomberg*, May 2000, p. 83)

Any front-line, routine job can be made more interesting and meaningful. All you have to do is ask the people doing the work what they wish they could

---

Dr. Paul Hersey, codeveloper with Ken Blanchard of the Situational Leadership method, points out that "Followers' performance often mirrors the expectations their leaders have." If you expect people just to do their work and go home, that's all you'll get. If you expect them to take an active interest in their work and strive for excellence, then you will get a great deal more!

–PAUL HERSEY,
SITUATIONAL LEADER
(WARNER BOOKS,
1992)

do, then figure out how to make it possible for them to do it. Usually this involves what the experts call "vertical job loading" but common-sense leaders like McDermott see it simply as letting each employee do some whole, meaningful chunk of work—and giving them enough training and support to make sure they can do it well.

Help Employees Deal with Criticism Positively

As a leader, you need to give employees accurate information about what they have done wrong and its consequences—and give this news fast. Sometimes, you will notice that the negative feedback discourages them to the point where they don't seem likely to take positive action to learn from the mistake and do it better next time. This method adds a positive pat on the back and some encouragement at the end of the negative feedback (not the beginning please!). You can end by asking them for their ideas on how to improve (which affirms your belief in their ability to do so), by encouraging them to fix the problem, even just by smiling—a nonverbal form of positive feedback. Here are some simple scripted examples (from *1:1 Leadership*, Alexander Hiam & Associates).

- The way you _____ed the _____ did not work out well because it caused a problem with the _____. I think you can figure out some way to avoid that kind of problem in the future. [Smile.] Any ideas?
- I think your _____ had a few problems. Specifically, _____. I think you can clean it

> The most effective leaders actively avoid making decisions that any of their people could make instead. Because they aren't always thinking and talking about decisions, they have much more time and effort to spend listening to their people and encouraging *them* to make good decisions.

up if you put a little more time in on it, okay?
[Wait to make sure they really agree, then,]
Thank you! [Smile.]

- This doesn't look right. It should be _____.
Can you fix this? [End with smile.]

These are direct corrections in which the manager does not hesitate to point out a problem or error. Often there is nothing wrong with that, but managers may hesitate to do so for fear of seeming rude. It helps to practice giving this straight delivery of the "bad news" in a polite manner, with a friendly, encouraging smile at the end to let them know you believe they are capable and competent in general, in spite of the specific problem. This approach does not sugarcoat the negative feedback—that would just make it harder to "taste" or actually understand. Instead, it delivers it right up front so the meaning is clear and immediate, then it uses a very simple, brief ending to let the employee know you are negative about the specific behavior but positive about them in general.

By the way, if you don't really think the employee knows how to do the task better, then you'll need another approach. You will need to add to the end an offer to help or provide support. A question like "Is there something I can do to help?" is the simplest way to do this. Be careful not to set an employee up for future failure. Sometimes it's not the person who needs correction, it's the task.

Don't Follow Praise with "But..."

Most managers know they need to provide positive feedback and praise, and in fact believe that they have. But ask employees and you get a different story.

The boss is critical. S/he doesn't appreciate us. Why the disparity?

Aubrey Daniels (founder of Precision Learning Systems) believes it is because managers can't resist adding a little advice to their praise. It usually goes like this: "Good work on that report, it was one of the best I've seen. Just one thing though, if you could summarize the financials in a short table up front it would be easier to read."

The boss's intention may have been to give praise and add a little helpful advice for future improvement. But to the employee, it sounds like the praise was just a warm-up for the criticism. So watch out for this easy-to-make error, and don't let a but or other qualification destroy the positive feelings of the praise. There is a time for corrections and improvements. And there is a time for praise and gratitude. Daniels' point is that they never overlap.

Make Negative Feedback Impersonal and Informative

So what *does* work? There is plenty of research indicating that focusing away from the individual and his or her qualities is important in negative feedback. *Don't* personalize it is the best advice (yet the sandwich method does make it personal). Also, it is quite clear that the more you emphasize information about the performance and its result the better. Be informative: "This is what happens when you do it that way, while you get this better result if you do it that way."

The alternative is to be controlling and manipulative, whether you mean to be or not. "I value you, you messed up but do what I say, and you may yet be

> **D**on't "sandwich" criticism of an employee's performance between an opening and closing that sounds positive. This might make you feel better about giving negative feedback, but it confuses the employee who will always be looking for the negative "filling" whenever you approach them in the future.

Try not to "store up" negative feedback!

successful here" is a sandwich of negative feedback within positive, also a controlling, manipulative approach.

Instead of using the sandwich, try to be factual, informative, and impersonal by focusing on the action or process and the results—not the person's worth. Then you won't have to worry about trying to wrap false praise around criticism. You can just focus on what went wrong and how to correct it next time.

Criticize Fast and First

Here's another approach to correcting employees that addresses a common leadership problem: It is tempting to delay your negative feedback because you're uncomfortable giving it. But delay reduces clarity and usefulness of the feedback. "Padding" criticism with up-front pleasantries sets up a negative emotional reaction so avoid that too.

Unfortunately, many managers never get around to giving regular feedback, especially regular negative feedback. They store up negative feelings until they are increasingly frustrated and negative in their view of an employee. Of course the employee seems oblivious because he or she lacks the feedback needed to recognize and improve upon poor performance. To avoid these problems, make sure you give negative feedback and any other bad news fast and first, before you find yourself padding the news to avoid having to be the bearer of bad tidings.

A Successful Intervention

A team leader in a manufacturing firm didn't know what to do about her "problem employee," a man

LEGAL PERSPECTIVE

Performance Problems

A positive approach to workplace leadership emphasizes what employees do right, not wrong. Managers might, for example, focus on praising good behavior instead of criticizing bad work—hoping to reinforce the good as a way of eliminating the bad. This can be effective, but there is a hidden trap in it. Avoid giving a poor performer only positive feedback because this creates an inaccurate impression of their performance that may cause trouble later on.

What if performance does not improve and the employee is terminated—and then turns around and claims he or she was fired because of age, race, or some other illegal reason? The manager's positive feedback will then bolster the claim that the employee was performing well and did not deserve to be discharged.

The basic preventive strategy in any such case is to document the performance problems. For instance, after an initial verbal coaching session, should the problems continue you need to write them up clearly and make sure you communicate them accurately to the employee (keeping a copy for the record). This does not prevent a positive approach to coaching for improved performance, it just makes sure you have an accurate record of any performance problems in case there is a need to refer to the documentation later.

When documenting performance problems, describe why the problem is important to the company. State the specific problems in terms of desired performance and actual performance. Consider the impact of the problem on your overall objectives, employee morale, or customer image. Also, explain to the employee how you expect the problem to be corrected. Be specific. Finally, give the employee a chance to explain his or her side of the story.

—NANCY L. O'NEILL, ESQ. OF THE NATIONAL LABOR
AND EMPLOYMENT LAW FIRM JACKSON LEWIS

with important technical knowledge but a bad habit of talking endlessly in meetings. He never seemed to take the hint and was driving the whole team crazy. The solution proved happily simple. She took him aside and told him clearly and with no sugarcoating that she needed him to change his behavior in meetings so that others could have more time to speak. She then asked him if he was willing to try to respond to questions or make comments within a specific time limit—emphasizing that she needed his expertise and knew it was difficult to discuss technical subjects in a succinct manner but hoped he could rise to the challenge. They agreed to a goal of three minutes per answer, and in future meetings she simply had to give him a quick raised eyebrow and smile if he started to go over this limit. Within a month he was "self-policing" and she no longer had to remind him to stick to the point and be succinct. (She did have to thank him though, to let him know she appreciated his effort to make the meetings run better.)

Strive for Measurable and Fair Rewards

Texas Instruments, like many firms, used a bonus program to compensate its sales force. In theory at least, salespeople could earn good bonuses for successful selling. The problem was that many of them considered the bonus program subjective and felt the bonuses paid were not directly enough linked to the skill and effort of the salesperson. What that does is create a strong disincentive by making people feel they are not treated fairly. It also clouds their view of their own work, making it harder to see when they are doing good work and reducing the quality of feedback and the resulting potential for learning and improvement. When feedback is not specific enough, quick enough, or enough to control through the employee's own efforts, it damages the employee's motivation by making it unclear how they can generate good results. That's a common problem with sales incentives as it turns out. And that may be why Texas Instruments is so pleased with its revamped bonus program, which was designed to be based on clear, accurate measurements and to be more driven by the results employees produce. These changes helped make the bonus program a better (read more useful and motivating) form of feedback for employees.

Put Employees in Charge of Their Own Reviews

Instead of telling employees how they are doing, Susan Gebelein of Personnel Decisions International recommends asking them to be in charge of their own performance reviews. Employees can collect information about how they are doing from multiple sources (i.e., peer and supervisor interviews, information systems and other internal records, perhaps even customers). Then instead of the manager running the performance review session, the employee "summarizes the information and leads the discussion of the review with the manager."

(From a *legal perspective*, you want to make sure poor performance is still documented somehow—maybe in brief memos to the employee reminding them of what is expected. Don't sugarcoat inadequate work or you will find you lack documentation should push come to shove.)

> "The day soldiers stop bringing your their problems is the day you stopped leading them. They have either lost confidence that you can help them or concluded that you do not care. Either case is a failure of leadership."
>
> —GENERAL COLIN POWELL, U.S. SECRETARY OF STATE

In U.S. Army training exercises, it is now customary for each leader to debrief the group afterward by asking them what they learned. A few minutes thinking about the experience can lead to a lot of insights into how to avoid mistakes the next time.

Ask Employees What They Learned

A good idea from consulting firm Best Practices LLC is to ask employees to do a "lessons-learned review" after each project is completed. After completing their assignment, ask employees to meet and identify the best and worst things about the project and come up with recommendations for how to do it better next time. It doesn't take long to add this learning-from-experience step to the work, and yet the benefits to both the company and the employees are potentially huge.

∪   ∪   ∪

Parting Thoughts

Supervision is a funny word. Because the first and lowest tier of management is called "supervisory" there is an unconscious urge to put supervision behind us and move up to the more impressive-sounding management or perhaps even to the ultimate status role, leadership. But supervision is not a level in an organization, it is a core leadership activity. If you delegate it to supervisors, then you better supervise those supervisors well or they won't be able to supervise your front-line employees well. There is no way to get around the need for supervision.

Going back to the horses again, think about the difference between a skilled rider and someone who doesn't know what to do and thinks you can just sit in the saddle and let the horse do its thing. Who is going to have a better trip? In spite of (or perhaps because of) their size, strength, and intelligence, horses need lots of input and feedback from their riders.

For instance the rider who wants to trot fast may "post" or move up and down with the two-beat movement of the horse instead of just bouncing around like a sack of potatoes. Riders learning to "sit the trot" need to learn to absorb the motion of the horse instead of letting it set up a contrary motion in them. Bouncing out of rhythm with the horse's movement results in bruises (for both horse and rider) and a counter-cyclical waste of energy that slows the horse way down by interfering with its natural movement.

Without good supervision, leaders and their employees run into the same sort of problems that inexperienced riders do. They find themselves bumping into each other at every stride and they have a worse and slower trip than if each had just gone on separate paths.

That is why both leadership and ridership are *active* endeavors. But there is a hidden trap in this idea to be careful of. When you find yourself bouncing uncomfortably, it is easy to jump off the horse and start running yourself—or easy to jump to the conclusion that your people don't know what they are doing and do it for them.

If you find yourself tempted to step in and take over, please remember that *it won't solve anything for the rider to get down on the ground and try to carry the horse.* The solution is instead to turn to the tools of good supervision and make sure they are being used at each and every stride, throughout your organization. Does everyone know what to do and why it is important? Do they have enough feedback to know how *well* they are doing those important things? Is the feedback arriving in forms that encourage learning

Not being an experienced rider myself, I was startled to learn that many riders give their horses constant verbal feedback. Talking horses may be a myth but *listening* horses are a definite reality.

> **G**ood riders know that their motion in the saddle can, if well coordinated, actually *add* speed and energy to their mount instead of subtract from the equation.

and improvement—not in ways that discourage, shame, or frustrate?

Finally, are they having *fun*? If so, this is a sure sign that the work is a worthwhile challenge that energizes your people instead of wearing them down.

Supervision Checklist

Here is a quick checklist highlighting some of the best ideas and practices from this chapter.

- ✓ Develop checklists to communicate key aspects of high-quality work.
- ✓ Ask employees to develop their own checklists of quality characteristics.
- ✓ Reward good performances with exciting new assignments.
- ✓ Never ask employees to compromise their personal standards.
- ✓ Encourage employees to find ways to conserve energy, materials, or time.
- ✓ Make sure employees are appropriately challenged with work that is neither too easy nor too hard.
- ✓ Give more support and structure for employees who are doing especially tough tasks.
- ✓ Let employees design their own performance reviews.
- ✓ Give your people opportunities to recover from hard work.
- ✓ Ask about each employee's most important assignment or goal.

✓ Come up with an improvement goal for your group.

✓ Expect the best—people tend to rise to your expectations.

✓ Find ways to recognize effort frequently.

✓ Give negative feedback in an informative and straightforward style.

✓ Make sure everyone has clear, frequent, and accurate feedback about their performances.

5

Innovation

> It is important to explore together. The best rides are often on unfamiliar trails.

Horses like to try a new trail on occasion. If confined to the same routine and environment for too long, they lose their enthusiasm and grow old before their time. It's the same with businesses, which need change and adventure to thrive. As a manager, you can run your horse along the same well-worn trail with blinders on it, or you can strike out into unfamiliar territory and break a new trail. Which one is going to be the better ride for you and your horse?

"On a recent trip to Hawaii, Nishimura bought himself a $2.95 bamboo flute and taught himself how to play. 'I'm

always curious about learning,' he says. 'It occupied me for about six hours. My wife thought I was nuts.'"

—KOICHI NISHIMURA, CEO, SOLECTRON
(*WORTH*, MAY 2001, P. 76)

The obvious reasons to innovate are good ones: cutting costs, finding new ways to land customers, introducing better products, improving distribution, embracing better technologies, and so forth. But there is more to it than that. The best reason is perhaps suggested by the comparison of businesses to horses. Like the horse, the business can easily get into a rut. Monotony and routine are its enemies. It grows stiff and inflexible. It stops looking around. It gets fat. And it doesn't have any *fun* any more. Will a horse like that win any races or achieve any other notable performances? Of course not, and we know in our hearts that businesses like that give unprofitable rides too.

Unfortunately the workplace can easily rob our people and ourselves of our curiosity, or at least make it hard to apply our creative imaginations productively and profitably. Innovating is perhaps the toughest assignment in the working world. Yet it is an assignment we all must take on in today's fast-changing, challenging business climate. If you aren't making waves you are liable to be sunk by them.

Innovation is sometimes associated with major engineering projects or new drug tests or other massive scientific endeavors. But in reality, innovations in what we do and how we do it are the daily lifeblood of every business. When the dust settles on any accounting

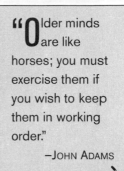

"**O**lder minds are like horses; you must exercise them if you wish to keep them in working order."

–JOHN ADAMS

The two most powerful engines of creativity are the questions, "Why?" and "Why not?" Unfortunately, they are asked far more frequently in the average kindergarten than workplace.

period the winners are generally the ones who had new ideas and figured out how to make them work. There is a greater need for practical innovation in the many mid-sized and smaller organizations than there is in even the largest companies.

As a leader, you certainly need to be thinking about new and better approaches. You need to be a *creative* leader, an innovator in your own right. But it is not enough to be an inquisitive thinker yourself, because you definitely need your people to catch the creativity bug too. It's a lot more fun (and profitable) when people make changes rather than resist them. Innovation needs to break out spontaneously all over your organization.

Let's see what people are doing to try to make that happen.

∪   ∪   ∪

Be Inquisitive

Leaders who have already made up their minds encourage their people to be closed-minded too. Leaders who are curious and interested in new ideas or questions spread creative thinking around them and stimulate innovation throughout their organizations. Inquisitiveness can take any form at all—even trying to figure out how to play a bamboo flute, as in the case of the CEO of Solectron, a company known for its innovative style.

Seek Inquisitive Employees

Thomas Edison is purported to have used the "soup test" in evaluating candidates for his company. He'd invite them over to dinner and watch how they

> "In the soft drink business, as a number two competitor in the market, you don't win by copying the other guy or by outspending him. You win by outflanking the competition with ideas that they would never think of or would shy away from if they did. Our innovation pipeline needs to be full for many years to come."
>
> –LUCIEN ALZIARI, VICE PRESIDENT OF STAFFING AND EXECUTIVE DEVELOPMENT, PEPSICO (*BUSINESS WEEK,* DECEMBER 17, 2001)

handled the soup course. Employees who thought-lessly shook salt or pepper on their soup before tasting it flunked the test since they weren't curious enough to find out how it tasted first. Those who tasted the soup enquiringly, then decided whether it needed additional seasoning, were more likely to get hired.

Staying Afloat in the Corporate Paper Chase

Norelco Consumer Products Company (a subsidiary of Philips Electronics) held one of its national sales meetings at the Marriott Harbor Beach Resort in Ft. Lauderdale, Florida. Taking advantage of the mild weather, sales managers formed the 100 employees into teams and challenged them to build seaworthy boats out of cardboard, tape, and other readily available materials. Employees who succeeded at this creative problem-solving exercise saw their next year's sales goals in a new light and were more likely to take a creative approach to achieving them.

A Persistent, Open-Minded Entrepreneur

Reading the obituaries is a great exercise for leaders who want to pick up a few tips from the recently departed. Take Al Greenwood for example. When he died in 2001, California newspapers ran lengthy stories on him due to his success as the founder, manager, and pitch man for a popular LA-based bedspread retailer. This specialized business made him a multimillionaire and a well-known character through his many appearances in TV ads as the "Bedspread King." (He gave humorous pitches for his

> Interesting exercise: Try to think of five ways to screen potential employees in order to find those who are most naturally inquisitive.

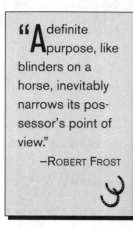

store from a golden throne, dressed in velvet robes and a crown.)

But how did Greenwood achieve his breakaway success? First, he was persistent. Remarkably persistent. In fact, his career didn't really get moving until he was in his 70s (and he continued to work into his 90s). Second, he was open-minded enough to try the idea of the Bedspread King ads out when a consultant suggested it, even though he thought it was stupid. Greenwood's idea had been to dress up for the ads as a cowboy, but he was sufficiently open to suggestion to give the "King" idea a try even though it wasn't his and he didn't think much of it. The rest is entrepreneurial history. It is also a good lesson for those of us still around to read the obit pages: business leaders who are sufficiently persistent and open-minded are far more likely to achieve breakthrough success than those who aren't.

Suggestion System Suggestions

Instead of just a box or other traditional "catch-all" system for collecting ideas, why not get specific and ask for the kinds of suggestions you know you need? For instance you could solicit ideas in categories like Saving Money, Retaining Customers, Conserving Energy, Reducing Inventories, Reducing Delays, Improving Quality, Attracting New Customers, Making Work More Enjoyable, and so on. If you ask for specific types of ideas you are more likely to get them. It's like inviting people to a party: invite ideas by name and they are more likely to come.

Idea of the Month

You could divide the year up into 12 categories of new ideas, and solicit suggestions each month in a different category. Then you could offer a trophy or other symbolic award for the best idea of each month.

How About a "Wild Ideas" Suggestion Box?

Take your ideas out of the box by offering a wild ideas box for those crazy whims that just might lead to something great down the road. Display or publish them in a newsletter or circulate them periodically by e-mail so everyone can tap into each others' cutting edge thinking. This way you can all tune in to the more wild and crazy thoughts in the organization—creative inspirations that are often hard to hear. (Better keep this suggestion box anonymous to loosen them up.)

Allowing "Free" Time for Thinking

3M is famous for allowing its people to spend up to 15 percent of their own time on "unofficial" projects of their own choosing. Innovations often come from these free-lance efforts. What if you don't run an R&D department at 3M? Does telling your people they can spend some time each week working on their own unofficial projects still make sense? It depends on whether your business is idea driven (or needs to be). If you need new ideas for improving customer service, cutting costs, speeding turnaround time, solving problems, or attracting customers, then you need to give your people the freedom to imagine. Of course you need to make the distinction between goofing off and inventing. You don't want employees staying home all morning then claiming they were "thinking." As long as they are genuinely pursuing some idea in the course of the work, let 'em go for it. The more

Are you encouraging employees to open their wings? *"A man who has no imagination has no wings."* —MUHAMMAD ALI

Please remember that creativity should be creative—not destructive. The point is to build something new of lasting value, not just to break all the rules. When Jeffrey Skilling, CEO of the ill-fated Enron, told his employees that "This organization believes in creative destruction."

—WORTH, MAY 2001, P. 73

He probably did not realize he was going to get what he wished for—literally.

LEGAL PERSPECTIVE

Inventions

When encouraging employees to be creative and inventive, remember to protect the company's proprietary interest in their inventions. If you send them home with an idea-generating assignment, it is possible for someone to argue that any ideas they submit were developed outside of the company's time and therefore belong to the employee, not the company. In general it is a good idea to have employees innovate with company tools on company time in order to protect your proprietary interest. Trade secret or proprietary information/development agreements may be appropriate for employees whose jobs require them to be creative and inventive.

—NANCY L. O'NEILL, ESQ. OF THE NATIONAL LABOR
AND EMPLOYMENT LAW FIRM JACKSON LEWIS

---

unofficial ideas the better. One of them just might prove profitable.

Start an Inventor's Club

The U.S. Navy's Carderock Division employs scientists and engineers who work on everything from underwater materials to propulsion systems. Although smaller than many such facilities, Carderock is a leader in number of patents generated and has a reputation for effectiveness. To encourage and recognize innovation, the division gives awards to successful inventors and also has an Inventor's Club. This seems like a good idea that could be used in any organization in which innovations are important. Why not start an inventor's club in your organization and accept nominations from employees to recognize any good idea that gets implemented successfully?

Send a "Virtual" Crawford Slip Around

Many years before e-mail was invented, Dr. C.C. Crawford came up with a clever way to generate good ideas on a topic. He had one person write an idea down, then hand the paper to another person, who added an idea of their own and passed it along. No talking was permitted because that tended to inhibit people's creativity. As a slip of paper circulated around a room, each person's idea inspired new ideas in the others until a large volume of interesting ideas was generated. While effective, this joint brainstorming method is rarely used because it can be a hassle to get a group of people together and have them all sit silently around a conference table jotting ideas on slips of paper and then passing them along. Most employees grumble when the rules of the method are imposed on them.

Enter modern e-mail. E-mail systems naturally make the Crawford process possible without any extra effort or hassle. All you have to do is to send an e-mail saying, "I need some ideas about X. Please jot down any ideas that occur to you, regardless of their quality, since one idea can lead to another. Then forward this to the next person on the list. When they have added their thoughts, they can forward it to the next person, and so on until it comes back to me. Thanks for your help." Add a list of all the people you want to include in your virtual thinking session and the e-mail will zip electronically through the list and eventually come back to you, having accumulated

Alarming but little-known fact: 99 percent of business e-mails communicate routine information. Less than 1 percent are devoted to trying to generate fresh ideas or innovations.

> **"If** a boss or organization is really acknowledging creativity, employees won't leave that place—even if the place down the street pays $40,000 more."
>
> —DICK DOOLEY, THE DOOLEY GROUP INC., RIVERWOODS, ILLINOIS

comments and ideas from everyone. If need be, you can circulate it another time for more ideas.

When you adapt Dr. Crawford's method to e-mail it becomes so quick and easy to solicit ideas and pass them along that there is no reason you can't do it any time you need a little creative input.

CEO for a Day

Employees at Cable and Wireless Optus in Sydney, Australia, held a lottery to select an employee and name a building floor after the winner for the year. Winners were memorialized with plaques showing their photos and names, describing their interests, and their answer to the question, "What would you do if you were CEO for a day? That's an interesting question, isn't it? Wonder what you'd get if you asked each of your employees to answer it. I wouldn't be surprised if you got some very good suggestions!

Feedback Fuels Innovation

"You need a continuing stream of feedback whenever you are really stretching. The Apollo moon flight was off-course 90 percent of the time...but Apollo had feedback mechanisms that allowed it to make rapid course corrections." Charles Garfield, author of *Peak Performance* (quoted in *Entrepreneur* magazine).

Opening the "Suggestion System" Books

Very few employee suggestion systems actually publish or make available all the ideas submitted. Why don't they? Why not make your system into an ongoing idea-generating dialog? After all, one idea leads to another—but only if the ideas are shared.

Engaging Minds, Not Just Hands

Nirvana Candles, a successful start-up in Freedom, California, has used modern ideas of flat organization and employee participation from the beginning. Employees are given lots of opportunities to expand their knowledge of the business and achieve job variety through cross-training and rotating assignments. They often take the initiative when it comes to upgrading equipment and improving production processes.

Support Self-Improvement Ideas

Giving work groups or teams the authority to actually implement their own suggestions can greatly improve the effectiveness of suggestion systems. For example, Palm Harbor Houses of Florida scrapped their suggestion box and asked each work team to gather its own suggestions for improvement instead. The only catch is that the teams have to implement ideas themselves. They are given a small budget of their own to play with, plus the option of requesting more funding if they think an idea is worthy of it. This system gets employees to think more practically and locally about improvement ideas, and leads to a lot more ideas being implemented than in a typical suggestion system. Employees really like being able to implement their ideas themselves instead of having to wait and see what management does or doesn't do with the idea.

Take the Lead by Visiting Employees to Ask for Their Ideas

To gather suggestions from employees who work for the state of Texas, the Texas Incentive and

> "Make sure you are feeling good before you try your hand at creative problem-solving. A positive frame of mind is essential! If you have trouble cheering yourself up, just try to make someone else feel good instead. Helping others is a sure-fire way to help yourself feel better too."
>
> —*UNLOCKING THE CREATIVITY CHEST* (A WIZARD'S GUIDE BOOK FROM ALEXANDER HIAM & ASSOCIATES)

Productivity Commission hit the road, visiting employees at their places of work to present information about how they can get involved and even to offer fun rewards for ideas and suggestions submitted to them. Apparently the program—called Destination Innovation—works well. The state reports savings of many millions from employee suggestions so far. There is something fundamentally appealing about going to the employees to seek their advice, instead of expecting them to come to you.

Respect Ideas to Make Improvement Contagious

An automotive supplier in Michigan achieved breakthrough results when several of its manufacturing plants reduced the amount of waste they produce by 90 percent in two years. How? According to the manager of the effort, broad-based employee involvement was the key—and it occurred because employee ideas and suggestions were taken seriously.

> *"It seemed like one good suggestion triggered two or three new good suggestions. Once people learned that their ideas were valued and would be considered seriously, participation... required virtually no stimulation. The excitement of making the Holland Plant more productive and more profitable, as well as making it cleaner and safer, seemed to be contagious."*
>
> —MEL SCHAUB, RECYCLING COORDINATOR, UNITED TECHNOLOGIES AUTOMOTIVE ENGINEERED SYSTEMS DIVISION (FROM A CASE STUDY BY THE MICHIGAN OFFICE OF WASTE REDUCTION SERVICES)

Ask Questions that Awaken Inquisitiveness

All innovations and good new ideas start with someone being inquisitive and sticking their nose into things. The capacity to question and wonder is blunted by the hustle and bustle of the workplace, and so it falls to leaders to try to reawaken inquisitiveness. In this method, all you do is make a point of asking inquisitive questions designed to spark creative thinking in your people. This not only models the desired behavior, it also demonstrates you are open to it—thereby giving permission for your people to be inquisitive and opening the door to their natural creativity. Here are some examples of appropriate questions (from *1:1 Leadership*, Alexander Hiam & Associates).

- What do you mean?
- What do you think about _____?
- I didn't know you were interested in ......
- Tell me about it.
- Do you have any ideas?
- Do you have any more ideas?
- Do you know anyone who might have some fresh ideas?
- Who do you think would be best for that project?
- Can you help me with this problem?
- Can you think of any additional options?
- Do you know anything/anyone that might be helpful with this problem?
- Can you think of any other ways to solve this problem?

Don't Be Afraid to Innovate

Telephone company Telus Communications in Alberta, Canada, has a staff of 500 operators who are members of a union. Recently the managers of this group introduced open-book management practices, sharing information with all employees and encouraging them to get more involved in management decisions.

> **W**hen people
> have fun at
> work, they are
> more creative and
> inventive and
> more self-
> motivated as well.
> A certain amount
> of horseplay is
> essential to a
> healthy work-
> place!

- What do you think caused this problem?
- Is there a better way to do this?
- Why do we always do it this way?
- Why can't we do it that way?

Encourage Playfulness

People are more likely to come up with good ideas when they are interacting in relatively unstructured ways, and also when they are having fun. Play stimulates creativity. So seek ways to inject opportunities for casual play in the course of the workweek. Relatively unstructured opportunities to play are probably better than the more common and highly publicized formal events and contests you often hear about in workplaces. What you want is the adult equivalent of the doll or building block—materials that invite imaginative play rather than structuring what you do.

For instance, some companies set up break rooms or creativity corners with art pads and markers, clay, "found" objects from nature like rocks and pine cones along with glue and boards to mount them on, drums and other simple-to-play musical instruments—anything that invites imaginative interaction with the material and/or those around you.

Here's another option. You can pick up some gerbils at a local pet store, along with clear plastic components that can be made into elaborate mazes and runs, giving the animals a simulated tunnel environment. The creative part comes in supplying the components and allowing employees to take charge of building and periodically redesigning the structure. You could even give an assigned week in which they create a design to anyone who wants it, then have all participants give out awards for best designs at the end of each quarter. Yes, it's silly, but silliness often stimulates imagination and initiative.

I also think an office kitchen supplied with basics for baking cookies, quick breads, muffins, or other office snacks can serve this same purpose, since cooking can be a very creative activity. Really, any activities that involve creative acts are good stimulants for the imagination.

Here's a Serious Approach to Work-Time Play...

Install a miniature golf course in the office and encourage employees to leave their cubicles and play together.

Well, why not?

That's what Illinois-based Lipschultz, Levin and Gray, a successful accounting firm, recently did. They installed a miniature golf course right in the middle of their office. Why? Well, nobody was talking to each other. Everybody was hunched over their own piles of work. The idea was to get people talking and cooperating more. They also wanted to introduce an element of fun. Does it work? According to company representatives, revenues are way up and employees are more enthusiastic about their work—and about golf, too.

Here's an extension of the idea. Why not get the basic building blocks of a miniature golf course, but let employees set the thing up and redesign it when they get bored with the old layout? Now you are stimulating a lot more creativity along with the play.

I've always fantasized about doing this with a model train set in the office—and letting employees have fun configuring it to their wishes, maybe even

Can you find any room in your workplace for a "creative corner" where people can go to refresh their imaginations?

using it to deliver memos or coffee...whatever their imaginations might suggest.

Understand and Manage Creative Roles

Please don't be fooled by the creativity stereotype, which says that some few artistic, imaginative people are capable of great creativity and the rest of us aren't. In truth, all inventions and innovations in business arise from a combination of this stereotypical "artistic" creativity style and several other styles combined.

It takes more than a wild imagination to innovate successfully. It takes other kinds of thinking too, including the disciplined, systematic style that gets things done and implements good ideas. As a leader, you need to recognize who has what creativity style in your group, and make an effort to mix them up so that any important project or team effort benefits from a healthy assortment of creativity styles. That way, you know you've got enough depth on the team to carry the project all the way through the complex creative process, from imagination to effective implementation.

Recognizing Different Creative Roles

To help you lead innovation, use the following guide to identify your own and others' creative roles. It is based on descriptions of how people think about innovations or how they tackle problem-solving (my firm calls this Creative Roles Analysis when we do it with clients). Which of the four descriptions best matches you?

1. *The Entrepreneur* recognizes needs and initiates the creative process. Thinking style is imaginative

but also systematic. Inquisitive, curious, independent, enthusiastic, motivated, takes initiative, sees possibilities.

- *The Artist* imagines possibilities and expands the creative quest. Thinking style is highly imaginative and not very systematic. Imaginative, enthusiastic, original, intuitive, expressive.
- *The Inventor* focuses the quest by seeing how to make the imagined possible. Thinking style is disciplined but also fairly free. Persistent, imaginative, determined, resourceful, focused.
- *The Engineer* completes the quest by ensuring successful adoption of the new idea or design. Thinking style is disciplined, focused, and systematic. Careful, goal-oriented, methodical, highly focused, and consistent.

Building Good Creative Teams

Now that you know what your creative style is, you know which role you tend to play too. (Are you an entrepreneur, artist, inventor, or engineer when you approach creative tasks?) This means you also know which roles you won't be likely to play. So now you can select employees or associates to work with you who will be naturals for filling the other three creative roles. Creative teams built of people with complementary role tendencies are usually quite effective.

Avoid "Bribes" for Creativity

Research on creativity shows that rewards for good ideas actually dampen the imagination. Apparently innovation and creativity need to flow from within

Which is your creative style—what role do you naturally tend to play in the creative process? Are you an entrepreneur, artist, inventor, or engineer? Do you have complementary people around you who can play other roles well too?

> **W**arning! Usually we are attracted to people with the same creative profile as our own since we understand how they think. Most creative efforts lack balance as a result.

> **"O**ne idea leads to another. Start with one and turn it into 100. Then throw away the worst 99."
>
> —*UNLOCKING THE CREATIVITY CHEST* (A WIZARD'S GUIDE BOOK, ALEXANDER HIAM & ASSOCIATES)

and be sparked by genuine curiosity. Trying to make it happen in a heavy-handed way by offering rewards for the best ideas is not going to work as well as one might think. (In other words, you can lead a company to creativity, but you can't force it to drink.)

Do Recognize Creativity

On the other hand, leaders who acknowledge creative thinking do get more creativity in their groups. Showing that you appreciate efforts to think out of the box is important. Otherwise your people will interpret your lack of attention to creativity as a sign that you don't want them to think for themselves.

Try saying "Thanks for the ideas" or "Interesting suggestion, keep thinking!" And how about asking for creative ideas during conversations and meetings? The leader who is open to brainstorming and invites people to associate from one idea to another is much more likely to actually get good ideas from his or her employees.

Acknowledge the Value of Stepping-Stone Ideas

Most of the ideas your employees generate are not ready for prime time. Yet many of them are good stepping stones that may lead on to better and more practical suggestions. As a leader, you can encourage the creative journey by recognizing stepping stone ideas and encouraging people to continue laying the path.

One way to do this is to simply say when you hear an idea that you don't like, "That's a great stepping-stone idea. Where can you go next with it?" This sure beats saying, "That's stupid" or "That won't work." It only takes one or two put-downs like that to dry up the idea well for many employees.

Innovate in Pairs for Maximum Communication

Developing any complex new product, project, process, or design is tough because it requires coordination of many tasks by many different people. Usually the parts don't fit together seamlessly and much debugging and extra work is required before the thing is really ready. This is nowhere more true than in the development of new software, which may be why a recent study by the Standish Group revealed that 84 percent of software projects are delayed beyond their deadlines.

That's not true at Evant Solutions in San Francisco, where software is developed by tightly knit teams of 10 or 12 people who work in groups or pairs and codevelop each part of a program. They communicate more than most development teams, uncovering and solving potential problems early on. They may even coordinate their work schedules to make sure they arrive and leave and eat lunch together during the development process so as to make it a true team effort.

The lesson for innovators in any arena is that the more tight-knit and cooperative your group, the more likely you are to have rich communications throughout the project—and thereby avoid many of the conflicts and problems that can sabotage a project near its end.

A creative journey of a thousand ideas must begin with a single idea. Hopefully nobody will step on it before the journey can begin!

Parting Thoughts

"It's important to have humility and realize that the people doing the jobs have the solutions."

—GERALD CHAMALES, CHAIRMAN, RINOTEK COMPUTER PRODUCTS (CARSON, CALIFORNIA; INTERVIEWED BY *THE WALL STREET JOURNAL*)

"People like to work in an environment that is fun, energizing, and where they can make a difference."

—KEN BLANCHARD (IN HIS INTRODUCTION TO *FISH!*)

Can You Top This One?

One man, an employee at Parker Hannifin Corp. in Cleveland, Ohio, appears to hold the world's record for most suggestions accepted by his company. His name is Urban Bianchi, he is a machinist, and at last report he had provided more than 800 ideas for cutting costs in his company. (Sounds like a classic "entrepreneur" in his creative role, doesn't he?) If Parker Hannifin only saved an average of $1,250 per suggestion, he still would have saved them over a million dollars. In fact the total is probably a great deal higher.

Here's a modest contribution to creative thinking in the form of two take-away questions you might enjoy chewing on.

- What would it take to spread this kind of creative enthusiasm to all of your employees?
- How much would your organization profit if you did?

Innovation Checklist

This checklist highlights some of the best ideas and practices from this chapter.

✓ Upset your own apple cart—seek ways of improving or replacing everything.

✓ Be inquisitive and encourage curiosity in your employees.

✓ Hire creative people who ask questions.

✓ Give other people's ideas as much thought as your own.

✓ Let people spend some time exploring ideas of their choosing.

✓ Ask people for their ideas by e-mail.

✓ Ask "dumb questions" to get people thinking.

✓ Recognize and thank people for their creativity—whether you like their ideas or not.

✓ Manage the mood of your group. Nobody solves tough problems when they feel discouraged.

✓ Keep a public record of all suggestions.

✓ Visit employees to ask for their ideas and suggestions.

✓ Encourage playfulness.

✓ Give strange ideas serious consideration.

✓ Recognize that different people play different creative roles.

✓ Recognize creativity but do not use controlling incentives and rewards.

✓ Learn from failures (instead of playing blame games).

✓ See if you can stimulate creativity through a suggestion system that breaks Urban Bianchi's record!

6

The Workplace

The best horses seem to come from the nicest stables. Horses spend a lot of time away from their riders, and if they spend it in a good environment they are more fit and eager to ride than if they don't. The wise rider puts a lot of effort into keeping the stall clean, getting the horse out on a pleasant pasture, and making sure it interacts with other horses so it does not become lonely or morose. The environment matters!

> To take care of a horse, sometimes you must clean its stall.

"Men and women want to do a good job, a creative job, and if they are provided the proper environment they will do so."
— BILL HEWLETT OF HEWLETT-PACKARD

You don't have to do all the leading and inspiring yourself. You are busy, and perhaps not always in the best of moods. But leadership does not have to be only about you and what you do. You can also let the workplace itself do some of the leading and inspiring for you. Why not create a working environment that naturally tends to turn people on and bring out the absolute best in them? (Even better, why not ask your employees themselves to create and maintain such an environment?)

The environment we work in includes the physical aspects, along with the other structures and policies that shape how and when we work, who we work with, and how comfortable and pleasing our workspace is. These factors have a huge influence over us, and yet most businesses and business leaders give surprisingly little thought to the working environment. They fail to manage it on a regular basis—which means they pass up a tremendous source of leadership leverage.

As you read the following collection of ideas, tips, and tools, you will perhaps be surprised at how many ways there are to put the workplace itself to work for you and your employees. For instance, something as simple as giving people more control and choice in how they set up their immediate workspace can create added commitment and drive. Any *time* flexibility you can offer is also highly valued by employees and tends to give them a greater feeling of personal control in their working lives—which may translate to greater initiative and responsibility.

Even something as simple as the color of a wall or the presence or absence of artwork, light, or moving

Creating an inspiring work environment means doing more than buying a poster and sticking it on the wall.

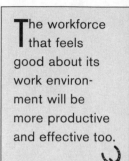

The workforce that feels good about its work environment will be more productive and effective too.

water can have a big influence on how people feel at work.

Special people and special performances seem to be found in special workplaces. You can inject this "something special" into a group of people by helping them create a special place to work. Let's see how some leaders have approached this opportunity.

∪   ∪   ∪

The Ultimate Perquisite: Privacy

Most employees work in a public space. From their workstations or cubicles they can hear and see others all the time, and others can see and hear them. Most people like a lot more privacy than that—or else they'd choose to live in communal houses instead of private apartments. If you want to help people make their workspaces better, give them the option of solid walls and increased privacy, even if it is only for a small portion of their working time.

Even a one-foot extension panel on top of the cubicle walls can make a big difference in morale. You can also encourage them to use tall potted plants, cloth hangings, or anything else they can find to increase privacy. (Soft materials absorb sound, which is an unnoticed but powerful source of stress and tiredness in most workplaces.)

"Shhh"

The average workplace has too much noise for good health or focused work, yet most of the time people are unaware of this according to a recent study by Gary W. Evans of Cornell University. He subjected one group of clerical workers to typical "low-intensity noises" like typing, phones, and conversations. Another group worked in quiet. Neither group reported any stresses or problems when interviewed.

The group in the noisier environment, however, had elevated levels of the stress hormone epinephrine, had trouble focusing on their work, and did not make appropriate adjustments to their chair and computer screen. In other words, the group with low-level noise around them suffered a range of negative effects. This suggests that workplace leaders need to take a proactive approach to minimizing background noise, even if employees don't complain about it. More barriers, textiles to absorb sounds, and greater separation of meeting and work areas are simple things you could do to get started.

When Outfitting New Space, Think Walls not Cubicles

According to Strategies Development Group, a corporate facilities consulting firm, it is not as expensive to build individual offices as you might think. A hard-walled office might cost more in building materials and time to create, but the free-standing office furniture needed to outfit it is usually much cheaper than good built-in furniture for a cubicle workstation. When the dust settles, the private office usually costs only 10 percent more. So if you are outfitting new space, don't assume private offices are beyond your reach.

Offer *Both* Private and Public Space

Employees who do knowledge work (that's most of 'em these days) generally work in spaces that are

Calient Networks (a San Jose, California, high tech firm) maintains a simple recreation room for employees to use as a stress reliever. It has Ping Pong and foosball tables and other basic activities that, at a minimal cost to the company, get employees moving around, laughing, and forgetting some of their anxieties and stresses, at least for a little while.

> In most workplaces, virtually no imagination goes into designing or modifying the work environment to meet individual needs. Why do we assume that the only legitimate workspace concepts are the ones sold by the "cubicle companies" or designed by architects? Just so long as safety is not compromised, employees can and should have a hand in shaping their workspaces.

an unhappy medium—their workspaces are semi-private, with small cubicles and offices that fit only one or two people, but also lack privacy for individuals who need to concentrate alone. Ideally, workspaces should provide quiet, private places to work (even if they are very small), combined with comfortable common spaces where employees can gather for teamwork or social bonding. When Adobe Systems moved into a new building in San Jose, it divided the floors into small walled offices and, at the end of every corridor, informal lounges where employees could gather. That way they have the choice of either working in private or coming together in a larger, comfortable setting. Even if you aren't constructing new facilities, you may be able to juggle things around in order to give your employees more private workspaces, along with a common area or lounge to encourage them to work in larger groups when appropriate.

A Maximum Flexibility Approach to Employment

We hear periodically of flextime plans where individuals can shift their daily working hours to fit their needs (daycare schedules, outside activities like volunteer work or courses, etc.). But HSB Bank PLC of London illustrates the point that you can take this idea a lot further than most employers do. They offer paternity as well as maternity leaves, part-time as well as flextime options for employees, and job-sharing schemes that allow hundreds of their workers and managers to perform important full-time work by sharing it with another person and thereby working half the normal hours. There is also a Family Leave option in which employees can take up to five days off to care for a sick dependent. The bank even offers what they call Career Breaks, allowing employees who have left within the past five years to have priority in reapplying for work. All this adds up to an incredibly flexible work environment that makes it very easy for employees to adjust their work to fit their needs.

Why? First of course, retention is improved since employees are more likely to stick around if their schedules are more convenient. Second, it improves the quality of their effort since people work harder and better when they can work on their own schedule. It means they feel more in control of their work and that they are not having to worry about what they ought to be doing instead of working. Third, being flexible is considerate and caring, something that most employees wish their managers would be—but don't usually think they are.

Encourage Employees to "Get a Life"

O'Neill Pine Co. of Beaverton, Oregon, is unusual in that it uses a 30-hour workweek and also allows employees to choose when they work those 30 hours. Employees find the flexibility and extra time for family life appealing and their turnover is extremely low as a result.

Keep It Simple

If you don't have the time and money to put an architect to work making things more inspiring, why not ask employees for some simple, practical ways of improving their environment? You could circulate a request such as the following: "Can you think of any ideas or suggestions for making our work environment more a fun, colorful, and inspiring? Please post

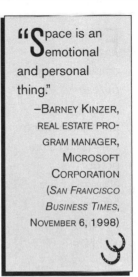

"Space is an emotional and personal thing."
—BARNEY KINZER, REAL ESTATE PROGRAM MANAGER, MICROSOFT CORPORATION (*SAN FRANCISCO BUSINESS TIMES*, NOVEMBER 6, 1998)

Examine each wall, floor, and ceiling. If any are dull, dirty, or otherwise depressing, *fix them*. A can of paint, a strip of cloth, or a colorful poster can reset the emotional climate quickly and easily.

Forty-four per-cent of employees say *bureaucracy* is the single greatest barrier to their being more productive according to a survey by Meaningful Workplace.com.

LEGAL PERSPECTIVE

Dealing with Disabilities

Many legal claims arise over how managers deal with employees who have injuries or other disabilities. Employees who feel they have been terminated or prevented from advancing as a result of any disability have many legal options. Managers can minimize their risks in this area by avoiding unnecessary disclosures from employees. There may be no real need to explore the employee's health in the first place, for example. But if an employee comes forward with information about a disability covered by federal or state law, the employer may need to make a reasonable accommodation to enable the employee to perform the essential functions of the position, provided the accommodation does not create an undue hardship to the company.

—NANCY L. O'NEILL, ESQ. OF THE NATIONAL LABOR
AND EMPLOYMENT LAW FIRM JACKSON LEWIS

---

all suggestions (whether serious or not) on the message board." Or you could ask a team to collect and act on the suggestions, letting them redecorate the office.

Working in the Garden of Eden

At Cisco Systems' United Kingdom offices, the more than 2000 employees are offered an unlimited supply of fresh fruit in the workplace. This simple symbol of support and appreciation may be one of the factors leading employees to vote this Uxbridge-based facility the best place to work in the United Kingdom.

Create a Great Place for Great People to Do Great Work

Marilyn Carlson Nelson, CEO of Carlson Cos., is often quoted as saying, "We call what we're

If you want people to take initiative and be innovative, then you need to give them a workplace that stimulates these qualities. A highly structured, uniform space does not.

doing creating a great place for great people to do great work." The company's philosophy is to invest in relationships with employees and build a loyal employee base, so that those employees will build similarly strong relationships between the company and its customers. (And they truly do call their 190,000 employees colleagues at this privately owned travel and hospitality services business.) One of the measures of success for this strategy is that employees (sorry, colleagues) generally find it a good place to work. Turnover is low and the company often makes local top ten lists of best companies to work for.

Some of Carlson Cos.' efforts to implement its strategy are big and expensive—for instance the company recently opened an on-site childcare facility at its Minneapolis headquarters. But in other facilities, the company arranged for discounts from existing childcare providers since it wasn't practical to build their own facilities in smaller offices. Nelson also pushed through a new time-off policy making it easier to qualify for vacation and personal time.

A little less expensive but still positive for employees are the many gift certificates managers hand out to the TGI Fridays restaurant chain and sometimes for weekend stays at Radisson hotels as well. The company owns both these chains so presumably this perk is less expensive than it looks—still it does say "we're thinking about you" to employees. So do the occasional weekday barbecues in a local park and the daily access employees have to cafeterias in the headquarters office. (There is a big one with an impressive menu, plus a smaller one in the I.T. employee's building called the Megabyte.)

> "The employees I supervise have children, families, and things they have to do. Being able to take a laptop home, to and from the office, and sometimes maybe just working at home and being able to allow our employees to do the same, actually benefits Cisco."
>
> —WRAL RADIO INTERVIEW WITH A CISCO SYSTEMS MANAGER (MARCH 2, 1999)

> "**E**mployees should have a fun, colorful, and inspiring work environment."
>
> —GYMBOREE CORPORATION'S INSTRUCTIONS TO THE ARCHITECT DESIGNING THEIR NEW FACILITIES IN SACRAMENTO, CALIFORNIA

There are also many intangible aspects of the "colleague" philosophy. Nelson and her management team are, as their management philosophy suggests, people oriented. A key part of making your organization a great place for great people to do great work is to be the kind of boss great people will enjoy doing great work with. Employees feel they can e-mail senior managers, even Nelson herself, if they have a question. Employees often say they feel they have the support of their CEO—in fact, one was quoted in a *ComputerWorld* article as saying "she really has it as a goal for this to be a top place to work, and she is making the investments."

Let's Get Moving

Motivation is simply the urge to take action—in other words, it is energetic movement. Yet there is a startling lack of movement in the average workplace environment. If the people are the only animated element and everything else is still, then the people have to generate all the energy. To combat this problem of low-energy physical work environments and add a little energy people can tap into, you could introduce things that move in pleasant ways. Calder-style mobiles can hang from high ceilings or low-traffic corners. A fountain with an electric pump can be combined with some palms in the entry or the window of a commonly used hallway or lobby. Fish tanks can be sources of energy if they have an active school of neon-colored fish (but some tanks are more sleep-inducing than energizing—make sure there are things moving around in it!). Even an old-fashioned electric train set winding around the outside of an office can be fun and add energy. (Could you deliver special news by train? Hmm...) In cold winter areas, a fire in a fireplace serves the same role and tends to energize those who see it.

Remember that employees need to have personal control over their direct exposure to such things. Please don't install a continuously moving train set that runs through people's personal work areas. Instead give them the ability to turn moving things off or place them in areas that employees can choose to visit or walk through, but don't have to be in all day. While pets can add a lot of movement and interest to the work environment, they are only appropriate if *everyone* likes them. For instance an office cat will produce negative energy in employees who are allergic to its fur—they'll be angry instead of enthusiastic. Similarly, a bird feeder or hummingbird feeder can add a lot of positive stimulation to a window view or entrance area—but make sure employees don't have to pass *too* near since some people are afraid of birds.

Birthday Dances

At the Rock and Roll Hall of Fame in Cleveland, they have an after-work birthday party for each employee on their birthdays. It's not mandatory, but people come if they can because it's a good party...and the music is usually pretty good too!

Beat Boredom with Games and Contests

In some factories, call centers and other workplaces with repetitive jobs find that Bingo games, safety contests, and other game-oriented recognition and reward schemes are quite successful. Managers generally

Employees at Carlson Cos. feel they can e-mail senior managers, even Marilyn Carlson Nelson herself, if they have a question.

The best equestrians take the time to understand what is important to their horse. A well-treated horse is in a better frame of mind and more capable of "going the extra mile" when necessary.

Employees of Shire Biologics enjoy art on loan form Boston's DeCordova Museum, and can also visit or take courses at the museum.

assume that employees are participating for the prizes, but in truth it is more likely that they are eager to relieve the boredom and appreciate having something new to engage their attention. Any new participatory event or program can have this effect if it is somewhat complex or varied and especially if it requires any decision-making on employees' parts. A key leadership principle is to *make sure nobody is bored at work!*

Let Employees Decorate Their Own Walls

Decorating the walls in your office or other work area is a great way to make the space your own and increase your sense of ownership. Yet most organizations control the walls—choosing everything from paint color to hangings without consulting the employees. You can boost motivation and commitment very simply by *giving your people control of their walls.* Follow basic rules of civility (nothing goes up that someone hates or is offended by) but otherwise, why not give people complete control of what they look at on the walls of their workspaces? (Okay, I agree, if the wall is in a customer service area, you may need to have more strict guidelines, but in most workplaces there is plenty of private wall space available.)

People are more energized and take more initiative when they have more control over the appearance of their workplace.

Let Employees Start (and Use) an Art Collection

On the theme of giving employees control over what goes on the walls of their workspace, why not create a library of framed prints and other artwork for them to choose from? If you buy posters of paintings and photographs the cost is minimal, even to have them mounted on boards or in frames. A number of companies (including General Mills and Mary Kay Cosmetics) have serious collections of art that employees can dip into for decorating office space. Posters work just as well if your budget is modest, and they are inexpensive enough that you could encourage employees to do the acquisition—then they have control not only of what they choose to display but of what goes into the collection in the first place. Remember, control is highly motivating and generates initiative and creative problem-solving, so this is about more than making the workspace attractive (although that's worthwhile too, don't you think?).

What if you budgeted a certain amount each year for adding to an art collection and allowed each employee to have a turn at selecting the next purchase? If there are too many people to make that feasible you could let them work in teams, or alternatively, have an art lottery in which you draw employee names once a month and select two or three winners who each get to spend up to, say, $50 on art. They can buy individually or pool their money for a bigger purchase if they like.

Leading Through Reading

Encourage employees to read by building a lending library of secondhand and contributed books. (You could have a simple rule to maintain it such as: anyone who takes out a book must put another one in

If You Scratch Their Backs...

Google Inc., a search engine company in Mountain View, California, has massage therapists on contract to provide neck and shoulder massages for employees who've been working on their computers for too long. (Or how about offering employees back-rubs or massages for their birth-days?)

> How often do we remember to ask employees if they are bored? And, if they are, to ask them for suggestions about how to solve the problem?

its place at the same time. That way no formal record-keeping will be needed.)

Consider adding a professional development section to the library consisting of books on business or technical topics of relevance to your group's work. (If these are purchased new out of your budget you might want to limit them to on-site use to avoid losing them. Or you could have a clipboard where employees sign out titles for overnight reading so that anyone who wants to read a missing title can track it down.) You can also add subscriptions to relevant professional magazines or journals to be shelved in the library.

It's incredible that 99.9 percent of workplaces do not have libraries. You'd think that any workplace where employees are expected to act intelligently would at least make this basic investment in human knowledge and learning. But better late than never, right?

Let Employees Stage an Art Exhibit

I met Jan Casey of Casey and Associates Art Advisors in the rental gallery of the San Francisco Museum of Modern Art. She was selecting candidates for a company's walls from the thousands of paintings, prints, and photos available for short-term rental or permanent purchase in that gallery (I bet there are similar galleries near your business; also bigger libraries, especially university libraries, often lend prints). She shared some of her stories about how clients have boosted morale and created engaging workplaces by letting employees have a hand in selecting artwork.

> How often does the art on display in your workplace *change*? It may be unrealistic to expect people to be more flexible and adaptive than their workspace is.

One idea I really like is to let employees put on an annual art exhibit in the main entry or lobby or a well-lit corridor of your workplace. She has helped some companies do this by purchasing or simply renting fine art from top galleries, but has also worked on shows of local talent and shows of artwork by children in the community.

One show featured the artwork of homeless children—a local charity goes into shelters to offer art classes to them. There are as many ways and ideas as there are budgets, so don't be afraid to explore the motivating power of art in the workplace.

Outlaw Bullying (and don't do it yourself)

Many workplaces have at least one loud-mouthed, overbearing bully, someone who makes others feel bad by correcting them or disagreeing vociferously with their ideas. (Unfortunately, bullies are more likely to be managers than not.) Traditionally, the attitude has always been, "well, some people are more difficult than others, but you can't fire someone for being overbearing." New research says we'd better take a harder line.

Mika Kivimaki of the University of Helsinki has just published a study showing that victims of workplace bullies have significantly more chronic diseases, and that bullying raises absenteeism by 9 percent and hurts employee motivation and the quality of work. How widespread are workplace bullies? More than half of the employees interviewed for this study say there are bullies in their workplaces. As a leader, you need to keep one ear tuned to bullying and make sure you stamp it out before it can do any damage.

Connecting Employees

After holding focus groups of employees to learn more about what they wanted, the leadership team at Florida-based AccuData America began a company

> "It's exciting for us to showcase pieces of art by local artists that we otherwise wouldn't be able to afford."
>
> —ELIZABETH OUNANIAN, CONN KAVANAUGH ROSENTHAL PEISCH & FORD (LAW FIRM, BOSTON), REFERRING TO THE DECORDOVA MUSEUM LOAN PROGRAM

> **A**nn Coker at the University of South Carolina-Columbia discovered that people who are verbally abused suffer as many health problems and as much stress as people who are physically abused. You need to make sure no one has to put up with insults, hostility, or belittling language on the job.

LEGAL PERSPECTIVE

Disrespectful Behavior

Avoid "rude" behavior toward employees. Many times, employees who feel their supervisor has been rude or unfair to them end up pursuing legal actions. A manager who barks out orders or berates employees for their errors may feel he is treating all employees equally (equally rudely, but equally). However, employees who feel bad about this treatment may well see it differently, feeling that they are being harassed. Claims of discrimination can arise as a result. To practice prevention, it is not enough to be equally impolite to everyone, since that can lead to hard feelings, which can in turn lead employees to seek legal remedies. Often the best preventive strategy is a polite and respectful supervisory style. There is nothing wrong with telling employees what to do or what they did wrong—but please try to do it politely!

—NANCY L. O'NEILL, ESQ. OF THE NATIONAL LABOR
AND EMPLOYMENT LAW FIRM JACKSON LEWIS

---

newsletter, scheduled more get-togethers and company parties, encouraged groups of employees to do charitable projects, and held more meetings with all employees. It is interesting that many of the employees' "wish list" items have to do with fostering communications and increasing human contact within the company.

Some companies rely on more high-tech ways to connect employees. Bobbie Gaunt, Ford of Canada president and CEO, was refering to Ford's computers-at-home program when he said, "The Model E program will help to unlock the full intellectual and creative capital of our company. I can think of no better way to achieve this than by connecting every employee."

Ethics for Lunch

At HealthEast St. Joseph's (a Minnesota health care facility), management schedules regular brown bag lunches to which they invite speakers. Instead of focusing on business topics, these events get employees to think about and discuss values and social issues.

Also unusual is HealthEast's creation of an Ethics Center, which hosts visiting experts, and an Ethics Committee made up of volunteer employees, which meets every other month to focus on ethical issues and staff education.

Providing Facilities for Bicycle Commuters

Pentagon employees are encouraged to commute by bicycle. A Web site gives them information on routes, and locker rooms are made available for their use if they want to shower. The idea, according to a spokesperson, is to "save time, money, and sanity." Those are certainly things most employees value!

There's Something Fishy Around Here...

Workplaces are inherently stressful. Water is inherently peaceful. Balance this equation by bringing water into the workplace in as many ways as you can. Freshwater Software Inc., a provider of monitoring and management for e-business Web sites, has taken this strategy to an extreme. The Boulder, Colorado company started out with one fish in a tank as its mascot, then graduated to one fish per employee, and finally ended up with a fish tank and school of fish for each workstation. Everyone has their own fish tank and can choose what to keep in it. All that water bubbling

Anybody Need to Get Away from It All?

Consulting firm BORN (headquartered in Minnetonka, Minnesota) owns ten vacation cabins on a lake for employees to use. (I wonder if one's available next weekend?)

According to a KPMG survey, 76 percent of employees have seen illegal behavior in their workplaces in the past year.

peacefully away and all those colorful fish darting around make for a remarkably peaceful environment, giving employees the calm needed to deal with a customer's crisis or handle the peaks and valleys of their busy workday. (By the way, the company estimates the cost of a tank at $18 per month, which isn't bad.)

Let Your Leadership Bubble Over

Another great way to bring water into the office is with small-scale fountains. Garden stores now sell more and more of these basins with small electric pumps and some sort of spout or something for water to cascade over. Many people find them very relaxing and enjoy having them in the workplace. But some people find the constant trickle of a fountain's water makes them have to go to the bathroom, so give them the option of working out of earshot. (Seriously! This is a problem for some employees.)

Leadership Is Leafing Out All Over the Place

Also consider lots of green plants. They bring water into the workplace in a more subtle way by humidifying the environment. They also take in carbon dioxide and pump out oxygen. Add oxygen and humidity and you create a more pleasant, cool, calming yet energizing work environment. Yet most companies stick a few potted palms or fake ferns in the lobby to impress visitors and leave the employees' workplaces bare. I don't feel like that is very good leadership because it doesn't do everything possible to ensure a healthy, productive workplace that helps employees keep their cool.

Make Your Workplace an Oasis

A great way to get the benefit of water in the workplace is simply to drink it. Sounds obvious, but do your people have easy access to clean, good-tasting water? Most employees do not. (Many of the water coolers in commercial office and factory buildings dispense decidedly nasty-tasting water, don't they?) Another option is to squeeze a bubbler and bottle delivery service into the monthly budget and station it where employees can conveniently take a fresh water break. This is guaranteed to be more calming and healthy than a coffee, soda, or cigarette break too. Especially if you surround it with some potted plants. And a fountain. And maybe even a fish tank or two.

∪   ∪   ∪

Parting Thoughts

I found myself pleasantly surprised by how many ways there seem to be to improve the work environment as I compiled this chapter. I bet that if you and your employees sat down and made a list, you could top these ideas with many more of your own.

Improving the work environment is a worthwhile activity whenever spirits begin to lag or people seem to need reviving. For that matter, it might be worth doing once a month, whether you think they need it or not. This is a powerful influence that few leaders use fully or well. Once again, I think there is perhaps something we can learn from the management of horses. Even if the owner of a horse is not riding it, she still knows it has to be tended to each day. Unless the horse is provided with all the basic

When I visit a company I hope to see "signs of life" like green plants, a temporary art exhibit, a lending library, or moving water. They are indicative of a healthy, lively corporate culture.

FYI: In a normal climate, people need to have eight glasses of water a day to function at their best. Dehydration can temporarily reduce mental functioning and emotional control.

needs, its environment is kept clean and tidy, and it is brushed and cared for routinely, it will not be ready to run when you need it to. In business today we need our organizations to run most of the time.

Workplace Checklist

Here is a checklist highlighting some of the best ideas and practices from this chapter.

- ✓ Recognize the powerful influence of any working environment over those who work there.
- ✓ Give employees as much privacy as possible (if they want it).
- ✓ Try not to hover over people as they work.
- ✓ Provide a mix of private workspaces and public gathering spaces.
- ✓ Match people to workspaces that have the amount of noise and interruption they like.
- ✓ Give employees as much flexibility as possible in designing their work hours.
- ✓ Provide a "creative corner" where people can go when they need inspiration.
- ✓ Make sure the workplace has colorful and energizing areas.
- ✓ Provide fresh fruit, spring water, and other healthy foods.
- ✓ Provide fish tanks, mobiles, and other sources of movement in the workplace.
- ✓ Hold parties or dances on employee birthdays.
- ✓ Create a lending library of books.
- ✓ Encourage employees to select and display art.
- ✓ Create places and times for socializing.
- ✓ Bring water and plants into the workplace.

7

Transitions

> Manage the major events in your horse's life carefully. These are the times it needs you most.

Sometimes bad things happen to horses, sometimes good things happen too. Whatever the event, major changes are times when horses need people's help the most. They foal and raise colts. They get sick. They get stressed when they have to be moved to a new place. Horses' lives, like all lives, are marked by transitions, and they need extra attention and care at these times. Managers need to recognize that their organizations are living beings too and may also need special attention during times of transition.

"An adventure is only an inconvenience rightly considered. An inconvenience is only an adventure wrongly considered."

—G. K. CHESTERTON

Business is really just a series of adventures these days, since things happen so fast. It seems like leaders are almost always contemplating the next transition—or even worse, fighting their way through the middle of it with less advance notice and time for planning than they would have wished. In today's fast-changing workplaces, leaders must be masters of change, ready to introduce a new method or reorganize to cope with a new challenge or even to help with recovery from the latest crisis or disaster.

Organizations change, the owners change, the people change, the technology and processes and customers and products change. Well, not all at once, but certainly at least one of those changes has happened to you in the past year, right? If you don't manage transitions gracefully and well, your employees can easily go on the defensive, circle the wagons, and slow things down considerably. On the other hand, good leaders are able to turn challenges into opportunities to gain momentum and enliven their groups. Turned-on employees are more likely to view changes as exciting new challenges than threats or sources of stress. So one thing we can say for sure about healthy organizations (and horses) is that they are eager for change and often seek it out or stir it up instead of fearing it.

But how do leaders turn the inevitable turmoil into a positive instead of a negative?

To lead your people through change, you need to be more mindful of their needs for direction and security. Your other leadership skills all come to the fore because good change managers are great communicators, great at redesigning the work to fit the new circumstances, good listeners, encouraging and supportive, and more. They use all the other leadership skills in this book. And they also deal with some unique problems specific to business transitions (like how to handle a financial crunch that demands payroll reductions). There are also many leadership skills that are unique to the challenges of managing through tough transitions.

Sometimes you need to react to challenges and changes, and other times you see the opportunity to take initiative and *make* changes others will have to respond to. But whether you are scripting the current change or just trying to respond to the newest surprise with grace, you are inevitably leading your people through change. It is just part and parcel of being a leader, of being in business today. You can't possibly lead a group for more than a year or two without having to oversee some kind of major change. Let's see how great leaders make sure everyone stays in the saddle and retains their enthusiasm for work during the inevitable times of turmoil and transition.

∪   ∪   ∪

Move Fast Through Transitions

If you are overseeing a change, it might be wisest to step on the gas. PricewaterhouseCoopers surveyed leaders who had been in charge of an acquisition for

> **"It takes great commitment to change and an even deeper commitment to grow."**
> —RALPH ELLISON

their company, and learned that 89 percent of them said that in hindsight they would do it faster. Time spent in transition is wasted time during which employees are unsure of their footing, making it hard to focus on work. Everybody waits to find out what is going to happen. Don't keep them waiting. Get it over with and get everyone back to work as soon as possible.

Create a Sense of Urgency

Sometimes your role as a leader is to challenge people to recognize that the organization is at a turning point and that they must leave no stone unturned in their search for new solutions and approaches. To make it clear that change was in the wind when DaimlerChrysler purchased Mitsubishi Motors, Rolf Exckrodt of DaimlerChrysler brought the managers of Mitsubishi an unusual gift. He gave each of them a chunk of stone originally taken from the Berlin Wall. He had each of these rocks labeled with the words, "Leave no stone unturned." The recipients of this gift could have no doubt that he was serious about making changes and expected them to produce new solutions to Mitsubishi's financial problems. Whether they enjoyed their gifts or not, the message came through loud and clear in spite of any communication gaps between headquarters in Germany and the new acquisition in Japan. I guess that whenever a message has to be made completely clear and memorable, writing it in stone is a good idea. Heck, it worked in the Old Testament, and it can still work today.

Bouncing Back

This inspiring quote comes from a survivor of the World Trade Center disaster, the sales manager of a firm which lost its headquarters and some of its employees in the attack of September 11, 2001.

"It's been bizarre stuff every day. This is one of the times in your life when you're really going to be put to the test. It's been inspiring to watch the people who take the challenge and go with it."

—NICK WEBB, VICE PRESIDENT OF SALES,
BASELINE (ASSOCIATED PRESS, OCTOBER 2, 2001)

Be Guided by the Employee's Voice

When any organization goes through a traumatic event or troubled times, there is a tendency for the leaders to centralize authority and feel called upon to set the tone and speak for the entire organization. But maybe the leaders are not sure how to look at what has happened, how to come to terms with it. That at least seemed to be the case for United Airlines, which lost two of its planes in the September 11, 2001 terrorist attacks. What should the company say to reassure its employees and customers? What sort of attitude is appropriate and helpful in the aftermath? These are difficult questions for any leader. So United did something unusual: It asked its *employees* to speak instead. Working with ad agency Fallon Worldwide of Minneapolis, the company videotaped interviews with dozens of employees, then edited them into spot advertisements to air on national television.

It wasn't the original plan. The ad agency had written scripts for employees to read—consistent with the tradition of scripting the "official" response in times of crisis. But when they got to talking to employees, they realized that the employees' views were moving and well thought out (after all, they have to live with it in their daily work). According to an Associated

> **"People learn a new skill more effectively if they have repeated chances to practice it over an extended period of time than if they have the same amount of practice lumped into a single, intensive session."**
>
> –DANIEL GOLEMAN, *WORKING WITH EMOTIONAL INTELLIGENCE*, (BANTAM DOUBELDAY DELL, 2000, P. 271)

Press report, Bob Moore, creative director at the ad agency, says, "Once we started filming, it became apparent that what they had to say from their heart was much better than what I had written for them." This was an interesting finding, and one that probably applies in every organization during stressful times.

An added advantage of letting employees take the floor in these ads is it helped United employees speak to *each other* as well as their customers, in their efforts to move the healing process ahead.

Practice Makes Perfect

In the majority of business transitions, employees are expected to make some significant changes in their behavior. They are supposed to learn new tricks and do their work in new ways using new systems, equipment, processes, or philosophies. Their leaders always complain that they are resistant to these changes and don't seem to take the new instructions or training to heart. The problem is that you cannot expect to change behavior just by telling people what to do. Even a full day of training is not really enough to bring about successful and permanent change. If you want to change any aspect of employee behavior, plan on giving them *repeated, brief lessons and practice opportunities over an extended period of time.*

- Design a learning plan for your group that spreads training and checkups over multiple weeks.
- Try to devote the vast majority of the time to giving them hands-on practice, not lecturing them or giving them information to read or view on a monitor.

Practice makes perfect, but only if you give people plenty of opportunities to practice.

Don't Get Blindsided by Changes

Changes are harder or easier depending on how well you have anticipated them. (For instance, the investor who sells tech stocks before they tank is not upset by a stock market crash. But the one who doesn't see the writing on the wall runs into it…the wall, that is.) A simple but powerful technique is to use weekly staff meetings to "sniff the wind" for possible shifts or trends. In fact, every leader should take a few minutes to share anything he or she has noticed/wondered about and ask employees what they have noticed. That way you are actually looking for signs of change, which increases the chances of being prepared by an immense amount!

Provide Adaptable Leadership

Of course you can't make a horse drink. But you can and must *lead the way to water*. This is a key part of the leader's responsibility, and it is complicated by the fast-changing business landscape. Sometimes the oases we aim for dry up and we have to change our course. How quickly we recognize the need for change and roll it out into new goals for all employees determines how much water we are able to provide. Consider the following, an excellent example of a decisive action by a leader that saved his organization from the worst effects of a drought.

"In February [2002], a month before the recession began, Tom Siebel…logged onto his company's Web site to…review the sales force's forecasts for the quarter. For

> "Later that same day, Hem and Haw arrived at Cheese Station C. They had not been paying attention to the small changes that had been taking place each day, so they took it for granted their Cheese would be there. They were unprepared for what they found."
>
> —SPENCER JOHNSON, IN *WHO MOVED MY CHEESE?* (G.P. PUTNAM'S SONS, 1998)

> If you don't take the time to look for *influence strategies* you will always be running. Sometimes you can get in the driver's seat—or at least do a little back-seat driving.

the first time, the figures had suddenly stalled." (Carleen Hawn writing about Tom Siebel, founder and chief executive of Siebel systems, a multi-billion-dollar sales-automation software firm, in "The Man Who Sees Around Corners," *Forbes*, January 21, 2002, p. 73.)

Siebel discovered that many of his firm's customers were postponing or canceling orders, and deduced that an economic downturn was coming. He quickly began slashing costs, revised his firm's projections and budgets, and asked his salespeople to rush the close of pending orders before those could get cancelled too. His was one of the few tech firms to anticipate and prepare properly for the recession that followed. The *Fortune* story goes on to explain how Siebel uses his firm's intranet to set overall sales goals, which are quickly rolled out to individual goals for all 1,500 salespeople. Then it explains how Siebel used this goal-setting system to change directions when he saw that a recession was looming:

"Siebel jumped on the intranet, retracted the 16 growth objectives he had placed there weeks earlier and replaced them with three simple and devastatingly clear ones: Keep customers happy, keep cash coming in, and protect market share. 'Everyone knows the goals and how they fit in,' he says."

Ask Your People If You Can Alter the Future

When something bad happens or seems about to, most people either freeze up like a rabbit in the headlights, or start running on the assumption they have to respond to the change. But what if you can alter the course of the car instead of having to get out of the way? Often we have more control over the course of events than we think we do. It's wise as a leader to stop and ask employees to consider whether there are any practical ways to alter the coming change even slightly so as to lessen its negative impact or possibly turn it into a business opportunity.

Day-Offs Instead of Layoffs

In the sharp high-tech downturn of Spring 2001, many high-tech firms announced cuts to their payroll—in other words, pink slips for many employees. Such layoffs are good for the short-term cash flow, but not so good for morale. Some companies preserved jobs by spreading the financial pain more evenly. They asked all employees to take mandatory days off instead. For example, Adobe Systems, Inc. closed all North American offices for a week in July, requiring employees to take four unpaid vacation days following the July 4th U.S. holiday. Figure it this way. One week saved out of 52 in the year for Adobe's 2,000 employees is roughly equivalent to firing 40 people or 2 percent of their workforce. A week off is the financial equivalent of a mild layoff, but not nearly as disruptive. If you find yourself in the position of having to figure out what to do to trim payroll costs, consider the Adobe model. Layoffs carry a lot of hidden costs and should be avoided whenever possible.

The Responsibilities of Leadership

A lot of business leaders reacted charitably in the aftermath of the World Trade Center disaster, temporarily suspending the pursuit of profits in order to help people who were in need. But leaders who had

How civil is your workplace? Consulting firm Envisionworks surveys employees with questions about how people treat each other. If they aren't very nice, the company gets a low score on the Organizational Civility Index. Civil treatment turns out to be especially important during times of change or stress.

never given much thought to civic responsibilities before sometimes found it difficult to step up to the challenge. One of them, the head of a New York head-hunting firm (which matches candidates to job openings for a fee), found himself and his company in serious hot water when *The New York Times* broke a story detailing his reaction to the human suffering resulting from the attack.

The news story detailed how one of this firm's employees, a young woman, had lost her husband in the destruction of the World Trade Center. Returning to her desk a week later, she was surprised to find that her boss had given some of her territory and accounts to others. When she asked what was going on, she was escorted to the president's office and told she no longer had a job. The story ends with a quote from the employee: "That people can act like this, that they think they can kick people when they're down, is so unbelievable. Would it have killed them to wait?" (*The New York Times*, October 4, 2001, p. A24)

LEGAL PERSPECTIVE

Employee Privacy

Careful who you communicate information about employees to. Employers may have a right to communicate information (such as the report of a co-worker that the employee acted in a threatening manner)—but only to those who have a need to know. That could include other managers or the police, for example—but certainly not a newspaper reporter or an acquaintance you see that evening at a party.

–NANCY L. O'NEILL, ESQ. OF THE NATIONAL LABOR
AND EMPLOYMENT LAW FIRM JACKSON LEWIS

No, it obviously wouldn't have. Nor would it have killed them to keep her on the payroll even if the weakening economy required them to make some lay-offs. Sometimes the circumstances require business leaders to step up and do the right thing. Like it or not, business leaders are *leaders,* and when people are in need there is a clear obligation to use the power of that leadership position for the better good. This is perhaps one of the hardest lessons for leaders to learn.

Focus with the Profitable/Successful Rule

What are your key criteria for success—and how well do each of the hundreds of things on your own and your employees' to-do lists relate to those criteria? I bet most of the to-do items aren't really very relevant. But they still clutter up the agenda and pre-occupy your employees. The CEO who oversaw the merger of video-conferencing firms VTEL Corp. and Compression Labs used a simple technique to focus his employees during the integration of the two organizations. He rated every agenda item according to (a) its financial impact, and (b) its probability of success. Most of the things on the to-do list didn't hold up to this scrutiny and were put off. The ones that rated well—they were both likely to be profitable and likely to succeed—got full attention.

Considerate Layoffs

Conventional management wisdom says to keep your cards close to your chest and play it tough when you have to do layoffs. The assumption is that employees are going to be angry and resistant so you

> "When I care to be powerful—to use my strength in the service of my vision—then it becomes less and less important whether I am afraid."
>
> —AUDRE LORDE

> **"The future belongs to those who believe in the beauty of their dreams."**
> —ELEANOR ROOSEVELT, U.S. FIRST LADY, 1933–45

> FYI: 64 percent of technology workers say layoffs at their company were unnecessary or too deep according to a recent survey, and two thirds of them distrust their employers now as a result.

better protect yourself. But Steve Kirsch of Propel Software doesn't see it that way. He felt bad about having to lay off 40 percent of his employees and was honest enough to admit it to the media (he even confessed to crying). He made sure the company did everything it could afford to ease the transition for them and the survivors left behind. He gave employees as big a severance package as he could afford, and more important, allowed them to make their exits gracefully by giving them continued access to their e-mail and voice mail accounts, accelerated vesting in the company's stock, and time to pack up, say goodbye, and leave on their own terms. News coverage in the local paper (*San Jose Mercury News*) quoted one of the laid-off employees as saying, "I think they did it with dignity and respect. They let you stick around and say goodbye to your friends instead of walking you right out the door."

(Caution: There are of course legal and security concerns in any layoff and you should obtain expert advice on them. However, also consider the power of prevention through creating goodwill instead of illwill in these difficult transitions.)

Another Alternative to Layoffs

Dennis Kozlowski, CEO of Tyko, needed to cut costs when the U.S. economy slowed down in early 2001. Rather than announce layoffs like many of his competitors did, he furloughed 5,000 employees in the electronics operations for two weeks and managed to avoid losing the talent and knowledge of existing employees. If you can make this strategy work, then when business picks up again you don't have to restaff—or rebuild trust.

Find Alternative Jobs for "Redundant" Employees

Conventional wisdom says that when you don't need an employee's job, you don't need the employee any more. For instance, when one company buys another and consolidates operations, much of the bottom-line benefit generally comes from eliminating some of the people who held similar positions in the two companies before the merger. But the CEO of Wells Fargo, Richard Kovacevich, disagrees. He tries to find other roles for employees after his firm makes an acquisition. He argues that by relocating employees instead of laying them off, his company has more experienced people who are more committed to their employer.

"Protect the Pot"

Norm Brodsky, an entrepreneur who went through a bankruptcy in one of his businesses after making it onto the *Inc.* 100 list, advocates a cautious approach to acquisitions, mergers, and other major strategic changes: "Through the agony of the layoffs, I developed a new understanding of the awesome responsibility CEOs have for the lives of their employees. Out of that understanding came the cardinal rule I use in evaluating every important decision I make: Always protect the pot. Once you have an ongoing, viable business, you have to put its welfare first and never do anything that would place it in jeopardy." (*Inc.*, July 2001, p. 32)

Encourage Exercise

Employees who exercise regularly (in activities of their own choosing) feel better about themselves and gain energy and self-confidence. According to a

The technology recession of 2001 hurt Intel of course, but CEO Craig Barrett didn't want to rely too heavily on lay-offs—so he started the cost-cutting by announcing that pay raises would be postponed for everyone, including the managers. In fact, he postponed his own raise too. Employees are inspired by people who lead by example, especially in trying times.

> **"I**f you don't think there's a correlation between happy employees and happy customers, you're missing a lot of data."
> –GORDON BETHUNE, CEO, CONTINENTAL AIRLINES (*WORTH*, MAY 2001, P. 87)

growing number of studies, exercise may be effective at curing depression as well. In fact, in one study at Duke University, people who exercised to cure their depression were doing significantly better six months later than those who received anti-depression medications. Not only that, but the patients who used exercise to treat depression did better than those who used a combination of exercise and drugs. Apparently the exercise regime made people feel better about themselves and more in control of their health and emotions because they had accomplished the cure on their own.

This is not to say businesses should stop offering medical care to employees who need it, but it does point out how powerful exercise can be in changing one's attitude and creating a more can-do, positive, and emotionally healthy perspective on life. Anything employers can do to encourage employees to pursue exercise is going to have a lot of lasting benefits.

Here are some simple ideas worth trying.

- Encourage people to bicycle or walk to and from work (or as a portion of their commute if they live far away).
- Recognize and communicate news about employees who do anything athletic. Have any mountain climbers or hikers, yoga instructors, polar bear club swimmers, triathletes, or kayakers done interesting trips on their weekends or vacations? Write them up in the newsletter or post a note about them on a bulletin board or your internal Web site.
- Consider offering health club memberships or subsidies as an employee benefit.

- In longer meetings, announce a circumnavigation break each hour, and lead the group on a walk around the building or block.
- Install a treadmill or stationary bike in the building.
- Ask employees to take turns leading a 15-minute stretching or exercise session each morning.
- Bring in a yoga instructor once a week and clear a conference room or hallway for a free class.
- Hold a mobile meeting, where each item on the agenda is considered in a different location and employees have to move from place to place by walking, jogging, or rolling.
- Form sports teams in recreational leagues in your area. (There are often adult leagues for sports such as volleyball, soccer, basketball, softball, and hockey. Ask people what they like to play.)
- Install a Ping-Pong table.
- Sponsor employees to participate in fundraising walks and runs of their choosing.
- Find a local facility that will let you rent time in their swimming pool and have a swim party there (please hire a lifeguard).
- Put in a supply of frisbees, juggling balls (or silk scarves for those who are too slow to keep balls in the air), beach balls, badminton racquets, and anything else you can think of. Encourage employees to entertain themselves in the parking lot, on the lawn, or even in the corridors. Movement and play are good for attitude, reduce stress, and increase flexibility!

Nerf is a great product for offices and workplaces because toys made from it are safe and need little room. Try nerf basketball in the corridors to get people's circulation going and raise their enthusiasm.

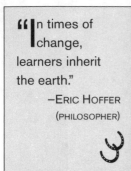

"In times of change, learners inherit the earth."

—ERIC HOFFER
(PHILOSOPHER)

Keep a Sharp Eye on Stress

Employees who are highly stressed cannot do a good job. They may not even be able to do their jobs at all. Usually managers do not worry too much about other people's stress levels, or even their own (although we should!). But during transitions and changes, there are a lot of extra stresses. Understand that these mean you have to provide more consideration for your people and give them more opportunities to relax and calm down and recover their normal equilibrium. Anything that helps counter the stresses of the workplace will help the transition go better. If you can't think of things to do every day and week to reduce stress, then ask your employees for ideas. Here are some simple suggestions to get you started.

- Screen a Friday afternoon movie on the office VCR, preferably a good comedy.
- Bring in someone who can lead 15-minute stretching sessions and encourage people to take a break every day.
- Go for a walk. Encourage others to walk too.
- Serve milk and cookies in the middle of the afternoon. It was a pleasant ritual in elementary school and it is still reviving today.
- For a more sophisticated break, institute tea time at 3:00 and put in a stock of regular and herbal teas (iced teas in hot weather) and small snacks. A 20-minute break with pleasant conversation can turn the day around and keep everyone sane enough to be productive for another day.
- Find some local charity and a way for people to do a little volunteer work—helping others generally helps us feel better ourselves.

- Ask employees to find the most calming, relaxing posters and offer to reimburse each employee for the picture of their choice (a $15 spending cap or something of the sort keeps this exercise from adding too much stress to *your* life).
- Order in pizzas, salads, or sandwiches for lunch.
- Take your direct reports out for an afternoon of miniature golf or other silly-but-relaxing adventures that involve physical movement but not the risk of injury.
- Introduce running water, green plants, and other calming influences to the workplace (see the workplace section of this book for more such ideas).

Remember that stresses on the home front add to those at work. Consider offering special half-days or hours off for employees who need the time to deal with personal issues. (See Chapter 3 for more ideas on stress management.)

Parting Thoughts

One thing that really struck me as I compiled this chapter on transitions is how the truly great leaders so often seemed to be the ones who *kept their humanity* during times of transition or crisis. They seem to reach deep down within and bring out the best in themselves and in others. They discover strengths and values they may not have known they had. I find that inspiring personally, and I wonder if you do too.

> **"To the body, there is no division between home and work; stress builds on stress, no matter the source."**
> —DANIEL GOLEMAN, *WORKING WITH EMOTIONAL INTELLIGENCE* (BANTAM DOUBELDAY DELL, 2000, P. 75)

FYI: According to surveys, 40 to 50 percent of employees are under significant stress at work. And that is an average workplace. Imagine how high the numbers must be in a workplace where significant changes are underway.

I don't have a lot to add on this subject myself (it is true I wrote a book on it once, but I am not sure that makes me an expert—I think it is something you really have to *do* to understand well). So instead I'm going to let some other people provide the parting thoughts for this chapter. Here are a few interesting quotes I really liked on different aspects of change and its role in business and in life—not to mention our role in it.

"Employees have the need for a deeper connection with their company during tough times."

—JOHN FARRELL, AN EXECUTIVE WITH
THE CARLSON MARKETING GROUP (*INCENTIVE*, AUGUST 2001)

"Major change never occurs successfully unless the need for change is obvious and the situation prompting the need is serious and fundamental."

—DAVID CARR, COOPERS & LYBRAND (ARLINGTON, VIRGINIA)

"As constant change becomes a way of life in organizations, the job skill with the biggest payoff is the ability to learn—and unlearn, and relearn."

—JOHN H. ZENGER, CHAIRMAN, TIMES MIRROR GROUP

"People always say that time changes things, but you actually have to change them yourself."

—ANDY WARHOL, ARTIST

Transitions Checklist

This checklist highlights some of the tips and techniques from the chapter.

✓ Look at the bright side. Changes create opportunities! Your positive attitude will spread to others.

"Don't swap horses when crossing a stream."

—OLD SAYING

✓ Don't procrastinate. Make changes fast once it is clear they have to be made.

✓ Look for ways to make each change a growth opportunity for as many of your people as possible.

✓ Recognize and support appropriate new behavior. Positive feedback is a powerful lever for change.

✓ Create opportunities for people to *practice* anything significantly new or different.

✓ Schedule a few minutes in each staff meeting to talk about trends and try to anticipate change.

✓ Seek ways to control or alter the direction of changes. You may have more influence than you realize!

✓ Cut costs creatively to try to avoid or minimize layoffs.

✓ Try to keep employees up and positive during change to avoid hurting customer morale.

✓ Encourage people to exercise.

✓ Make the case for change by sharing information on why it is necessary.

✓ Manage stress daily. Never stop thinking about it during a transition.

✓ Remember that employees need a deeper connection with their workplace in tough times. Avoid the tendency to cut communications and build barriers during transitions. This is when all your "people skills" are most important to good leadership.

✓ Encourage a certain amount of "horsing around." Humor is a great antidote to stress and, when appropriate and tasteful, often helps us shift to a positive point of view. As the leader, you probably should not be making light of any change that employees feel threatened by. But if *they* try to find the humor in it, by all means encourage them!

8

Encouragement

> Encourage your horse
> to believe it is a winner.
> It won't run its hardest
> until it does.

orses like to win races. It makes them feel good. They respond well to encouragement and praise. The winning trainer knows his or her first task is to make sure the horse feels like a winner. Star performances are produced by stars. Do they *feel* like stars right now? Without that belief, no horse can run its hardest and no business can achieve its full potential.

ᴗ   ᴗ   ᴗ

ast night I sat outside and watched a meteor shower. As the shooting stars streaked glittering down the sky, I thought, hey, that's just what I want my organization to look

> **P**eople's performances are strongly affected by our expectations of them. As leaders, we have to be careful to focus on expectations about what people can do right, not worries about what they might do wrong.

like—only in *reverse.* I visualized those stars all appearing faintly, low on the horizon, then shooting up to glow brightly in the heavens above me. (I actually feel very strongly about this idea, strongly enough to have made it the theme of my firm's logo, which shows a star above a curve. Our motto is "Helping achieve above-the-curve performance" and we endeavor in our own small way as a training source to help other organizations achieve star performances from their people too.)

A star shooting up is admittedly a very positive, affirming way to view your people. But is it realistic? Interestingly, there is plenty of evidence to show that people's performances are strongly affected by our expectations of them. Employees who are encouraged and told they can do great things *do* great things.

You probably recall hearing about those classic studies of students in which one teacher is told he or she has a group of brilliant kids with great potential and the other teacher is told his or her kids are losers. Invariably, the first group leaps ahead while the second group falters. Teachers may unintentionally produce stars or dropouts depending on how much they expect the children are capable of. Their behavior toward the children is so different when they think the kids have potential versus when they are focusing on what the kids do wrong.

I guess that it should have come as no surprise when the consulting firm Surcon International crunched its huge database of employee surveys and company results and found that profits were higher in organizations where managers were more considerate toward their employees. (See the appendix of *Motivating & Rewarding Employees* for details of this study.) Concerned managers who take a genuine interest in the people who work for them produce superior bottom-line results. But, BUT, as the president of Surcon pointed out to me when he shared those findings, most business leaders do find the result surprising and are resistant to the implications.

The problem is, we have a long, long tradition of leading people by telling them not to mess up and warning them what not to do if they don't want to get in trouble. As teachers and parents and managers we often find ourselves playing the role of a judge or cop instead of star-launcher.

For instance, if you actually keep a record of what a supervisor says to his or her people for an entire day, you generally find that the vast majority of those communications take the form of orders (what to do and how to do it) or corrections (stop doing that, why did you do that?). Traffic cops aren't leaders, nor are managers who spend their days directing traffic and handing out speeding tickets.

Yet our old habits die hard, and these old habits are ingrained deeply in our culture and business practices. All of us were managed by "traffic cops" much of our lives (starting in school!) and so it can be hard to break free of old role models and pioneer a new, more encouraging and positive style of leadership.

To achieve the star performances we need, we have to *believe* our people are capable of being stars—and start giving them star treatment now. That way, we can become star business leaders ourselves (yes, encouragement needs to begin at home—you can't belittle yourself if you want to build up others). Here's a look at some of the techniques and practices we can use to pioneer this new, encouraging style of leadership.

In *The One Minute Manager*, Blanchard and Johnson use the term "leave-alone zap" to describe a common supervision style in which the manager ignores employees for long stretches of time until something goes sufficiently wrong as to require correction—then the manager "zaps" the employee with a correction or other negative feedback. This seems to me to be management by negative expectation instead of positive.

> **"P**eak performers are not motivated by fear. Peak performers are not concerned about what you can take away from them."
> —HARRY CHAMBERS
> AUTHOR OF *FINDING, HIRING, AND KEEPING PEAK PERFORMERS* (PERSEUS BOOKS, 2001)

(Ahh, did you see that? That star just shot *up*. And there goes another one…and another.)

∪   ∪   ∪

You Have the Power

Here is a striking thought for any business leader:

> *"Studies on employees have shown that the greatest influence on job satisfaction is the supervisor."*
> —BOB NELSON (AUTHOR, *PLEASE DON'T JUST DO WHAT I TELL YOU! DO WHAT NEEDS TO BE DONE*)

In fact, this thought is a little bit scary when you come right down to it. It makes me wonder whether I'm having a positive or a negative influence at any specific moment.

Can You Find Something Nice to Say About Everyone?

Business leaders might want to take a page out of the Miami Hurricanes' playbook. This University of Miami football team has an annual award dinner at which it gives out a Most Valuable Player award…and 16 other awards too. The coaches use the opportunity to recognize almost every player instead of just focusing on one or two standouts. They do this by giving out awards for very specific things so that each award recognizes a real contribution of importance to the team. There are awards for commitment, work ethic, and even an "unsung hero" award. For a football team (or any team) to function well, everyone needs to be operating at a high level of commitment. The idea of recognizing everyone with a wide range of appropriate rewards is only fair, and it avoids the common problem of awards demotivating those who don't win them.

Encouraging the Troops

Jim Amos, former Marine captain and now president and CEO of Mail Boxes Etc., spends a lot of time recognizing and rewarding his employees, and believes this is part of the reason his firm has very low turnover and very dedicated staff. For instance he sometimes types letters of appreciation and mails them to his employees' homes along with a gift certificate for a local restaurant. Amos sometimes notifies local papers about notable things employees do, and also holds monthly "Eagle Renewal" employee meetings to applaud promotions, introduce new employees, give a monthly Eagle award to an employee, and announce the peer-nominated Soar Award for going beyond the call of duty. That's a lot of celebration compared to most companies, who might do something of the sort once a year at best. Amos explains, "In the military you [recognize and reward] with medals, awards, and letters of commendation, and these things carry over well into the civilian world." (*Incentive*, January 2002, p. 15–16)

Give Positive Feedback Before Success, not After

Almost all the recognition and reward schemes used in businesses are for a job well done. But heck, if the employee already did the job well, how much leadership is needed now? More important by far are the many employees who are in the middle of a tough

> **"Thanks cost nothing."**
> —AFRICAN PROVERB

task, and the many other employees who are doing something at least a little better than before, even if it isn't a great job yet. Your leadership can make a bigger difference if you refocus your recognition efforts on work processes and improvement efforts rather than the end results.

One way to make this subtle but powerful shift from recognizing successful end results to recognizing progress along the way is to shift your approach to recognition. Emphasize informal, frequent feedback to your people over fancy, occasional awards. Try saying things like "I appreciate the effort," "great effort," "looks like you're making progress," "go for it," "that's a clear improvement," or "we may have a lot to do still, but we're making progress."

It is a healthy habit to recognize progress toward a desired end result. It allows us to provide leadership along the way. When we hang out at the finish line and clap when the employees stagger over it we aren't being leaders, we're being spectators.

Practice Saying Thank You

How often do you thank employees for their effort? How often do you tell them you appreciate what they've done? Interestingly, most managers say they offer their thanks routinely. But most employees say they rarely if ever hear a sincere thank-you. What gives? Evidently, in spite of our best intentions, we don't always get the message across that we appreciate the good work, patience, initiative, ideas, effort, and many other contributions our people make. My hunch is that most leaders simply find it difficult to express their feelings fully and clearly in this area. Do you? Here's a simple test: how many ways can you think of in the next 30 seconds to say "thank you" to your employees?

I'll wait a minute here, if you'll just go ahead and make a list. Thanks!

Okay, good work. I appreciate your going along with me on this one. Now, how many different ways did you list? How easy or hard was it to come up with natural-sounding variants on thank-you that you'd be comfortable saying to your people in the daily flow of events?

This is actually a difficult exercise. And that gives us a telling clue as to why most employees don't seem to get the message that they are appreciated. It's a lot harder than it sounds to say thank you clearly and frequently. It's a difficult leadership skill, and that means it is worth working on. There is always room for improvement.

One way to expand your "thank-you range" as a leader is to write a list of all the things you want your people to be. (Imaginative, hard-working, responsible, helpful, careful, polite, collaborative, persistent, smart, creative, economical, resourceful, accurate, or whatever you think the work calls for.) Now, once you have your list of desirable employee attributes, come up with a recognition statement for each. In other words, practice thanking them for being careful, caring, supportive of each other, persistent in solving a problem, creative in finding ways to make do without having to buy expensive new parts, or whatever.

Get specific with your thanks. Thanking an employee for helping out with a problem is easy. Thanking another employee for working hard is also natural and easy. When you work from your list of desired traits, you'll find many natural opportunities

> "**S**hould you feel your energy lapsing, try this surefire remedy: Find someone who needs a helping hand, a word of support, or a good ear—and *make their day*."
> —ADVICE FROM *FISH!* BY STEPHEN C. LUNDIN, HARRY PAUL, AND JOHN CHRISTENSEN

> **"I** ask, 'How many of you say 'thank you' to your subordinates when you give them their [pay]checks?' Only one out of a thousand managers do that. The rest think I'm crazy."
>
> —FERDINAND F. FOURNIES

to recognize them in your people and to offer your thanks. Any leader who thinks showing appreciation for employees is as simple as repeating the two-word phrase "thank you" over and over is not communicating his or her appreciation as effectively as possible.

Tell Them You Appreciate Them

"CNN executives were surprised when Ms. Van Susteren decided to leave the network and did not want her to go. But they had paved the way, in part, by showering attention on the network's new star anchors…while depriving Ms. Van Susteren of the care and feeding top anchors expect, people close to the situation said."

—JIM RUTENBERG, "BEFORE GOING, VAN SUSTEREN TOLD CNN OF HURT FEELINGS," *THE NEW YORK TIMES*, JANUARY 28, 2002

This scoop by a *New York Times* reporter gave an insider's view of Greta Van Susteren's abrupt departure from a high-profile job at CNN to switch to a rival network, the Fox News Channel. Van Susteren also complained about discrimination and lack of diversity at CNN. She accused her former employer of putting corporate interests above journalistic ones. Such accusations (regardless of their specific merit) are common when an employee feels slighted or injured. When your feelings are hurt, you tend to lash out at your employer, and many employees take legal action in an effort to right the emotional balance. The root of the problem is often, as apparently in Susteren's case, "hurt feelings" and "feelings of neglect." Employees who feel that their contribution is not valued often look for work elsewhere, and hurl accusations and pursue grievances at higher than average rates.

Recognize *Sustained* Effort

NASA recognizes employees who repeatedly show exceptional effort and whose attitude is consistently positive over time with a special award called the Silver Snoopy Award. As the award administrator explains, "most awards in most organizations are for single achievements yet we need sustained achievement!"

Reward Employees with Meaningful Experiences

Quite a few companies are discovering the "secret" of resort/workshop destinations as incentives and rewards. Instead of offering a traditional trip to top salespeople, for example, why not offer a retreat at a fabulous resort that includes fun educational activities? That's what Terra Noble in Puerta Vallarta on the west coast of Mexico offers. You can cue up meditation, art therapy, massage, kayaking, whale watching, and other activities. You can even have a team of employees do developmental exercises that build confidence, creativity, and rapport. Or you could try something a little closer to home, like the Wyndham Peachtree Conference Center in Peachtree, Georgia, where there is a 19-acre corporate training facility offering forest adventures. Why not let your incentives and rewards strengthen your people, not just entertain them?

Don't Let Rewards Make People Feel Small

> *"If you doubt that rewarding someone emphasizes the rewarder's position of greater power, imagine that you have given your next-door neighbor a ride downtown, or some help moving a piece of furniture, and that he then*

Victoria's Destination Services, Inc. of Las Vegas arranged a dinner party for top salespeople of a printing company at which a magician entertained the guests, then offered magic lessons afterward.

offers you five dollars for your trouble. If you
feel insulted by the gesture, consider why this
should be, what the payment implies."
—ALFIE KOHN (*PUNISHED BY REWARDS: THE TROUBLE WITH*
GOLD STARS, INCENTIVE PLANS, A'S, PRAISE, AND OTHER BRIBES,
HOUGHTON MIFFLIN 1999, P. 28)

I've thought hard about what this story means to me, worrying at first that perhaps any and all rewards could take the genuine pleasure in being helpful away or might signal disrespect and a controlling, top-down style. I don't think so now, because there are plenty of situations in which people seem genuinely happy and honored to receive a reward. The trick certainly must be to put yourself in someone's shoes and imagine their response—and make sure that whatever rewarding you do is done in a respectful manner that honors them and makes them feel big, not small.

Candy or Praise?

In another blow for traditional "jelly-bean motivation" approaches, a researcher at Sonoma State University in California compared performances of people who were either given candy when they did well on a test or verbal encouragement. The encouragement helped boost performance next time, the rewards didn't. Specifically, the encouragement produced increased self-esteem and also better work performances.

However, the verbal feedback had to focus on the task at hand to be fully effective. If managers say something like "keep up the good work and you'll probably make supervisor next year" they have just added a complicating factor—performance anxiety and the fear that the manager is linking one's future somewhat arbitrarily to a specific task. So give encouragement—but keep it about the task at hand. (Research by Rebecca Shulak, reported in *Psychology Today*, January/February 2002, p. 16.)

Give Unsatisfactory Employees Options, Not Pink Slips

This idea comes from Paul Falcone, director of employment and development at Paramount Pictures in Hollywood, California. He sometimes has to step in to help resolve cases in which managers are unhappy with employee performance. Often the manager feels it is time to fire the employee and hire someone new. But there are costs to this course of action, including the unemployment benefits and the hard feelings which can bite back in the form of claims of wrongful discharge (when the employee argues that he or she was fired for no good reason or for a bad reason like discrimination) and constructive discharge (when the employee leaves voluntarily but claims that he or she was forced to do so because of poor treatment).

To minimize hard feelings, Falcone recommends letting the employee know that you know the situation is not good right now, and that the company is available to support the employee in the pursuit of multiple options to resolve the problem, such as:

- Making sure working conditions are acceptable and that objective performance criteria are given the employee if he or she wants to stay on and try to make it work, or
- Supporting the employee (e.g., with the necessary time off) if he or she wants to begin searching for another job.

Have you prepared your "joke of the day" for your employees yet?

Falcone emphasizes the importance of giving the employee options and being polite and supportive during the process. It's essential to make sure the employee can choose to leave with self-esteem intact. When he presents these options, a high percentage of employees end up leaving without hard feelings and it is rarely necessary to go through a difficult and more costly termination process. (See *HR Magazine*, April 2001 for more details.)

Spirit Booster

At a residential ward of a veteran's hospital, one of the nurses started the practice of sharing a joke with everyone in the daily group meeting. The practice became something like a ritual, with staff and patients insisting on a new joke every day. Now employees scour joke books and collect good jokes they hear from others to make sure there is always something new to use for their daily joke.

Birthday Parties

When I was little I assumed that every workplace must celebrate each employee's birthday. Maybe I just grew up (finally) last week, when I was shocked to see a statistic saying that employee birthdays are only celebrated with a gift or party in less than a fifth of businesses. It's a simple thing for each employee's direct supervisor or manager to organize a little party and offer some refreshments and a birthday wish. They might even give a small present on the company's dime. Consideration is a leadership essential after all, and it seems a small thing to give it by celebrating a birthday. Think of it as taking care of the child within us all!

Encouraging (the Right) Spirit

At Silicon Graphics, Inc., the goal is to encourage employees to take initiative, be creative, and fix problems instead of playing the blame game. Yes, I know you want the same thing, but at most companies, managers gripe that their people don't show the right spirit. At Silicon Graphics, management takes active steps to generate a good company spirit. For instance, once a year 50 employees are recognized with "spirit" awards. That is a lot of awards and a lot of recognition, so it sends a strong, clear message that spirit really matters. A spirit award gives management the opportunity to define and communicate their ideal for what they feel the company spirit needs to be, and then to recognize those who embody this ideal. It sure beats complaining about people but never doing anything to improve attitudes.

Who's In Charge of the Entertainment?

Phelps County Bank in Rolla, Missouri, gives work teams the task of deciding what to do with a company-sponsored hour-long break once a week. They have a budget and freedom to come up with anything that tickles their fancy as long as it is safe and doesn't offend anyone.

Remind People of Their Strengths

Whenever you encounter a situation in which it is appropriate to point out or probe for an individual's relevant strengths or competencies, you could take advantage of it to remind people of specific skills or abilities or past successes with statements or questions

> "We try to treat employees like customers, because like customers, if they don't like the way you treat them, they can walk."
>
> —MARK HANSCOM, OWNER OF AN AWARD-WINNING GYMBOREE FRANCHISE IN LAKE OSWEGO, MINNESOTA

> **"I've** never said a good manager shouldn't correct people when they deserve it. But just remember, every time you throw somebody down the stairs, you owe him four trips back up."
>
> —FRAN TARKENTON, AUTHOR OF *HOW TO MOTIVATE PEOPLE* (HARPERCOLLINS, 1986)

that remind them to focus on and apply their strengths. Some examples:

- That's a tough challenge. It's a good thing you have a lot of experience with these kinds of problems.
- Is there some way for you to take advantage of your knowledge of the _____ system when you tackle that project?
- You always seem to be good at getting cooperation on these sorts of things. Is that a good strategy for this project?

(From *1:1 Leadership*, Alexander Hiam & Associates)

And the Nominees for Best Supporting Team-Member Are...

Ever considered recognizing talented performances with your own version of the Academy Awards? That's what Viacom's Human Resources department does, starting with a peer nomination process and culminating in an elaborate award ceremony in which nominees and winners are given star treatment, from a cocktail reception and dinner through a real on-stage award ceremony complete with crystal trophies. Oh, and don't forget the employees who submitted nominations. At Viacom, they receive thank-you notes. Every employee participates in the event and is aware of the buzz that is created by posters, announcements, and preliminary events leading up to it as well.

By the way, a recent medical study found that *actors who received Academy Awards lived on average four years longer than similar actors who didn't*. I think this says something important about the value of recognition and how it contributes to a healthy, positive view of the self.

Participatory Variant on Academy Awards Ceremonies

I'm excited about ways to engage employees in the design of events like this. It will have much more power if volunteers do most of the creative work of designing the awards and the event. This tends to open up the possibilities for positive recognition, because now you can thank not only the winners but also the volunteers who made the award event happen.

Reward Employees with a Great Work Environment

According to David Russo, vice president of human resources at SAS Institute, "Recognition can come from more than just a name on a plaque. It can come through the environment you give your employees. The environment is in itself part of the reward employees get for working here." That includes nicely designed and maintained office space and a great many family-friendly benefits, like on-site child-care—one of the most popular rewards among SAS employees with children. (Visit Chapter 6 for more ideas on how to reward employees with a great workplace.)

Don't Forget the Lowly T-Shirt!

It's easy and inexpensive to have T-shirts silk-screened with custom-designed art and messages to commemorate any special event. Some companies

> "People who feel good about themselves produce good results."
> —KENNETH BLANCHARD AND SPENCER JOHNSON, *THE ONE MINUTE MANAGER* (BERKLEY PUB GROUP, 1983)

> "If only the manager or highest performer of a group is recognized, the group is apt to lose motivation."
> —BOB NELSON, *1001 WAYS TO REWARD EMPLOYEES* (WORKMAN PUBLISHING, 1994)

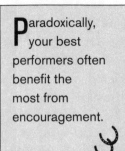

Paradoxically, your best performers often benefit the most from encouragement.

create T-shirts for events like a fun run or community service day. Others create T-shirts emblazoned with the names of project teams. Or how about a "SUR-VIVOR" shirt with a clip-art picture of a deserted island for those special employees who worked extra hours to put on a special event, handle a seasonal rush, or deal with a major initiative like a move into a new facility? Check your phone directory for silk-screeners near you. Many have artists on staff who'll help you with a design for a minor fee.

Parting Thoughts

I was reminded of an interesting point recently when I heard a presentation by Peter Schutz, the guy who turned Porsche around and who now does a lot of work helping and speaking to other CEOs. He asked the audience what they thought should be done about a poor performer. Not someone with an honest desire to succeed and a little temporary trouble, but someone who was clearly not destined to be a star in your organization, at least not this year. Such "problem" employees are highly likely to end up turning into the leader's greatest headache because they can be so hard to fix. Well, we in the audience came up with lots of positive ideas and a few tough ones too. Then Peter offered *his* suggestion, which was to *ignore them* as much as possible.

I was left sitting there with my mouth open wondering if he was for real. But his point is an important one and I think I now see the wisdom of his remark. The people who stick out as problems are probably not going to be your star performers. It's the quiet ones who don't cause trouble who usually have the star potential. If they are doing okay without any attention, it's tempting to keep ignoring them—and give your limited time and attention to the worst employees instead. That's a bit like training the slowest horses in your stable in the hope that you'll win a race. (Peter's advice might be to stop worrying about the slow horses and perhaps even start leaving their stalls open at night in case they get a notion to go to someone else's stable and slow them down instead.)

If you don't have the time to give extra attention to everybody, then I guess it's a good idea to allocate it to those who have the *most* potential to succeed, not those who don't. Good effort and good performance deserve recognition. There's a lot of star material to work with in most businesses and encouraging our stars is a good use of limited leadership time.

Encouragement Checklist

This checklist highlights some interesting tips and techniques for bringing out star potential.

- ✓ Encourage yourself. You can't build up others if you don't feel good about yourself first.
- ✓ Focus on strengths and potentials in the people who work for you.
- ✓ Find specific things to recognize or reward each employee for.
- ✓ Encourage people for trying hard. Don't wait until they have finished a job.
- ✓ Recognize progress, not just results.
- ✓ Say thank you often and in varied and specific ways.

✓ Reward employees with meaningful experiences (learning, travel, special events).

✓ Recognize the contributions of each individual, not just the group as a whole.

✓ Ask people to tell you about their contributions.

✓ Start a tradition of having a daily joke.

✓ Give a spirit award.

✓ Put employees in charge of the entertainment during a weekly break.

✓ Remind people of their strengths when they face challenges or problems.

✓ Ask people what their personal goals are.

✓ Find ways to recognize aspects of each employee that make them unique. Treat them like the individuals they really are. (How much do you really know about their interests, for example?)

✓ Celebrate all successes, even small successes. They are the stuff stars are made of!

9

Decision-Making

> Choose the right path and your horse's journey will be an easy one.

O ften the horse that completes a journey first is simply the one that took the shortest path. The rider's main responsibility is to make sure the horse goes the right way and doesn't get lost. However, the decision-making has to be a shared activity, since the rider chooses the path but the horse must walk it. Decision-making is a team effort in the workplace too, in which manager and employees each contribute their unique perspectives. Neither can make the best decisions alone. The best rider knows that sometimes their horse has a good perspective on what to do too.

"You can't do all of the thinking for everyone in your organization. Try it and you are sure to fail."
—WILLIAM A. COHEN, *THE ART OF THE LEADER*

Decisions, decisions. The life of the leader seems to be plagued by decisions. There are the all-too-numerous trivial ones that bog you down in detail. Then there are the big decisions where you have to stick your neck out and hope the future won't surprise you with a quick chop from the guillotine. Leaders need to not only make good decisions, the right decisions, but they also need to recognize which are the important decisions they have to get right, and which in hindsight are going to prove trivial and not worth their trouble. Making good decisions is itself a major task for any leader.

Then there is the issue of how decision-making affects your employees. As a leader, you probably try to see decisions as opportunities—opportunities to exercise leadership by involving people and encouraging them to develop responsible judgment of their own. That is a way that leaders turn on their people in the most successful organizations. When and how you engage your people in participative decision-making is an important consideration.

Both the decisions you make and the *way* you make those decisions are part and parcel of your leadership. To lead is, after all, to lead *to*. You always need to be going somewhere, to be moving toward a desirable destination (or, perhaps, away from an undesirable one). It's the same with riding a horse. It's a given that the horse has to be moving in *some* direction while you are riding it—but where?

Decisions are opportunities to get your hands on the reins and your feet in the stirrups—or perhaps to share the control with your employees. There are lots of ways to go about this, as the following examples and techniques illustrate.

∪   ∪   ∪

Distinguish Vision from Overconfidence

A few years ago the Sloan School of Business published a study showing that most managers suffer from overconfidence in decision-making. Specifically, they believe their guesses are more accurate than they really are—which means they may make risky strategic bets. Even scarier was the finding that this *overconfidence is greater the higher you go* in a business. Senior executives and business owners have the worst cases of overconfidence.

I thought of this study when the economy slowed down in 2000. Many of the dotcom start-ups failed of course, and overconfidence goes without saying when you look at their business model with the advantage of hindsight. But even in established businesses there was a lot of unrealistic thinking. Brad Mead, president of small business investment banking firm Delta Capital Group LLC of Avon, Connecticut, observed that his clients were ignoring the bad economic signs and their own declining sales—but still budgeting on the assumption that sales would *grow* in the next year. He told his clients (according to *Inc.* magazine), "To assume the downturn is only temporary is a pretty big bet. As a CEO, you can't take that chance." But still, many did.

> You'd have to be crazy to take a horse over a jump without having checked to see what's on the other side of it first. But for some reason it's considered acceptable to take blind leaps in business.

The lesson, according to Mead, is that many business leaders and certainly most entrepreneurs are optimists by nature and tend to look at the future through rose-colored glasses. That's great when you want to get everyone fired up about the potential for your business, but not when you are writing budgets or raising money to fund them. Then you need to consider multiple scenarios including some ugly ones to make sure your vision is realistic as well as exciting. Organizational survival is the first responsibility of the leader. Growth comes second.

So watch out for the "optimism trap" as Mead puts it. Leaders certainly need to think big, but they also need to protect the company.

Completion Is Key

"In the final account of what you do or don't do, you get 10 percent for planning and 90 percent for execution. Get the job done and tidy up the battlefield later. We must not get so wrapped up in artistry of the beautiful scheme of doing something that we discover that the train just left. The question we must answer is, 'What did you do for the Army today?—NOT, 'What did you 'plan today?'"

—MAJOR GENERAL ALBERT B. AKERS

Do We Rethink Decisions Often Enough?

"The chairman and chief executive of Providian Financial Corp., the controversial and financially troubled San Francisco credit card giant, said yesterday he will step down amid acknowledgments by company officials that a cornerstone of its business plan has been a failure." (*San Francisco Chronicle*, October 19, 2001, B1) In the end, the leader is the one accountable for the decisions. It's best to make sure plenty of thought goes into them and to reconsider them at every turning point along the way.

They say it's never too late to change your mind. But as the CEO of Providian learned, it might be wiser to say that *it is never too **early** to change your mind.* Sometimes the only way to find out if a decision is any good is to give it a try—and then turn around in a hurry if the evidence is unfavorable! The leaders with the longest tenure in business are usually the ones who don't mind changing direction frequently.

Don't Feel Pressured by Your Competition

Often everyone in a market or industry gets on the same bandwagon at about the same time. As a leader, it can be hard to go against conventional wisdom. As a result, you may often find your so-called vision is simply to do what everyone else thinks companies like yours should be doing right now. Margaret Whitman, CEO of eBay, showed a laudable independence of mind when she held back and refused to join the throng of dotcom companies spending huge amounts for prime time advertising before they were profitable. For instance, in 1999, her competitors went for multi-million dollar Super Bowl ads, but she held back and waited another year before launching her first big ad campaign. In hindsight, her prudence was warranted. eBay has survived and thrived while those early big spenders are mostly gone by now.

> **▲▲** [Bill] Belichick [head coach, New England Patriots, 2001–2 season] is proof that a man can change. ...The old Belichick probably would have mishandled the quarterback situation or the Terry Glenn problem... and even though the Patriots' defense relies on his concepts, he doesn't micromanage it."
>
> –*SAN FRANCISCO CHRONICLE* ANALYSIS, FEBRUARY 3, 2002 (SUPER BOWL SUNDAY), SUPER BOWL XXXVI

Plant Hay When the Sun Doesn't Shine

It's easy to follow the herd and profit when times are good or, as the old saying has it, to "make hay when the sun shines." It is harder to know what to do when it's raining. Should you pull back or keep trying to achieve your goals? Juniper Networks, a Sunnyvale, California Internet equipment maker, doubled its number of customers in the latest recession, even as the size of purchases plummeted and its operations posted significant losses. CEO Scott Kriens explained his strategy in a *San Francisco Chronicle* interview (January 16, 2002, p. B6): "We will not walk away from or under-compete in this market because of a business cycle."

Encourage Decisiveness with the "48-Hour Rule"

Most decisions and actions in any business require some input from others. Even in a small business, the employee may need to ask the boss if it's okay to do something. In any business with more than a dozen employees, nobody makes a move without getting input from at least one other person. The problem is, people rarely respond as quickly as they should. They may not answer a question for several days, if at all—leaving the decision-maker hanging and unable to act.

To solve this problem, Aperian Inc., an Austin, Texas Internet services company, introduced a radical rule: Any employee is allowed to make a business decision *without* someone's input if they don't hear back from them within 24 hours. That rule applies not just to peer input but also to an employee who asks permission from a boss to do something. This puts managers on notice that they better respond right away to any questions or requests from their people. It's a tough discipline but a good one once you get used to it. After all, if you aren't accountable to your people, how can you expect your people to be accountable to you? (*The Wall Street Journal*, March 6, 2001, p. A1)

Solicit Reservations Before Deciding

The captain of the nuclear attack submarine the Greeneville ordered the crew to surface rapidly in the waters off Hawaii on February 9, 2001—not knowing that a Japanese boat carrying college students was on the surface above the submarine. The Japanese boat, the Ehime Maru, was sunk in the ensuing collision and nine lives were lost. How does a submarine's captain decide whether the water is clear above his ship before surfacing? He relies on both sonar evidence and a visual examination of the area through the submarine's periscope. In this tragic case, however, the waves were high and the Ehime Maru was not visible through the periscope. Too bad there was no evidence from the sonar examination to warn the captain of the risk.

Or was there?

Subsequent investigations revealed that a crew member had actually made an accurate plot of the Japanese ship's location based on sonar evidence and suspected that the fishing boat was dangerously close to the submarine. But he did not question his captain's order to surface. He kept his concerns to himself. Even worse, a senior officer was on board and he said later that he thought the captain rushed the surfacing

If it's possible to sleep on a decision, do.

> **"Anybody know anything I don't?"**

drill—but he too failed to voice his reservations. If only the captain had simply *asked* if anyone had any relevant information before giving his order!

When you make important decisions, decisions you and your organization cannot afford to get wrong, take a little time to stop and ask people if they have any reservations. And consider using that specific word: *reservations*. It is a powerful word for surfacing concerns and comments. When you use it, you make it clear you are not asking them to make the decision or opening the thing up for a consensus process or a democratic vote. *You* are making the decision, but you want to check to *see if they know anything you don't* that could prevent an error. That's what you say when you ask if there are any reservations.

By the way, some groups are naturally more nervous and resistant to change than others, and will flood you with vague and groundless reservations that seem more like whining than legitimate concerns. Short-circuit this and focus them only on important issues by phrasing your request as follows: "Does anyone have any *specific* reservations about this course of action?" Specific reservations are ones that have some clear focus, some grounding in fact or at least probability. They are more likely to be useful to your decision-making process than general reservations. (It does you no good to hear "I'm worried something might go wrong" for example.)

Vision Is Great, as Long as the Trains Run on Time

Leaders are torn between the future and the present, between the big picture and daily minutia. If they focus too much on daily operations, they risk neglecting their role as visionaries who need to explore the strategic options and champion their organization's future. Yet if they are too hands-off and disconnected from current activities, they run another risk—their people may feel they do not care about the things the employees care about.

This is a universal leadership challenge, as illustrated by complaints against Tony Blair, when as Britain's Prime Minister, spent a lot of time working on foreign policy issues overseas. Blair's vision (in his words) was "to make Britain a worldwide force for good." Pretty exciting leadership stuff to be sure—but only if the daily details are also taken care of. Unfortunately, he got a lot of bad press at home as he jetted around the world in pursuit of his vision.

The British newspaper *The Observer* quipped that "History is something Tony Blair reckons takes place outside of Britain." (January 6, 2002) His press suffered even abroad, with *USA Today* quoting his people as saying things like "It would be nice if he could get the trains to run on time" and observing that "Britain's vital services—transport, health, education—have been woefully underfunded the past 50 years" and that "Blair's cabinet heads...are widely considered weak." (*USA Today,* January 10, 2002)

Leaders who manage to focus their time on big-picture issues without getting into trouble for neglecting the details are ones who have great people working on daily operations—ones they can trust to make "the trains run on time." If you don't have the luxury of trustworthy operational managers, then perhaps that is the first thing you should work on. Otherwise, you

> **"The only way to be successful...is to hire terrific people and point them generally in the right direction. And let them go. I don't run things, I lead things."**
> —STEVE CASE, CHAIRMAN, AOL TIME WARNER, INC.
> (*THE WALL STREET JOURNAL*, JANUARY 7, 2002, P. B1)

will always be torn between two full-time jobs: running operations on the one hand, and trying to build strategies and plans for a healthy future on the other.

Recognize and Reward New Business Initiatives

Berlitz International is a far-flung empire with over 300 language centers to keep an eye on. It has always rewarded those that made their numbers, but recently began to recognize and reward good new ideas and initiatives as well. Nominations are now drawn from each division for people or teams who have done something creative to grow the business. Winners in the first year of the program got $3,000 in cash, silver logo pins, and a trip to a special meeting at the Biltmore resort and spa in Phoenix, Arizona. Some of the great initiatives recognized include a new team design for managing customer relationships and a language course taught over the Internet. This kind of recognition encourages employees everywhere in the organization to make good business decisions and work together to implement them.

Create a Coalition of Leaders You Can Talk To

To make sure you never have to wrestle with a hard decision in isolation, approach other leaders and build a pattern of asking each other for input. For instance, if you own and run an independent retail store, you might call up a friend who is an officer in a local bank and ask if she would be willing to be a sounding board on occasion, in exchange for you doing the same thing. Or you could tap into local groups of business leaders such as you might meet at a Chamber of Commerce or Rotary Club meeting or at a meeting of a local chapter of a professional association. Some of them will be trustworthy and experienced and well worth including in your leadership coalition.

Start small, with the occasional question, and make sure you act as a sounding board for their questions too. Over time, it will get to be a habit and you will find it natural to pick up the phone and call one of these colleagues whenever you are uncertain about how to handle a problem or what to do. It is amazing how much easier it is to see the answers when it is someone else's problem, not your own. Perhaps that is why Jane Galloway Seiling of the Business Performance Group (in Lima, Ohio) reports that coalitions are "important resources in times of trouble," and that successful people tend to have "multiple coalitions that have developed over the years." (Quotes from *Performance in Practice*, Winter 2000–2001, p. 6.)

Quarterback Fran Tarkenton on "Participative Huddles"

I've never been real upset at being called a genius, so in my Viking days I didn't take out any ads announcing that the theory was a crock. Take this as a belated confession. All those sportswriters who said I was a fair to middling runner and passer but a top-notch caller of plays, take note: I called about 25 percent of our plays myself. The rest were called by 'lunks' like guard Ed White and end Ahmad Rashad, and my good buddy and roommate, center Mick Tinglehoff. When you stop to think about it, this is just common sense. Nobody can solve every problem,

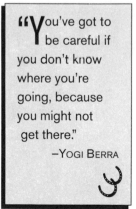

You've got to be careful if you don't know where you're going, because you might not get there."

—YOGI BERRA

every time, on his own, so if you're already working with a group, doesn't it sound pretty reasonable to find out what that group thinks?" (From Tarkenton's contribution to the gosmallbiz.com site.)

Foster Employee Involvement in Decisions

In general, managers and business owners tend to err on the side of too little employee participation in decisions. Participation increases big-picture understanding, develops employee knowledge and skills, and stimulates internal motivation. The more participation you have, the better (but see the legal perspective for a caveat; like almost everything managers can do, there is a legal as well as a management perspective on employee participation).

LEGAL PERSPECTIVE

Employee Committees

You want employee input, but sometimes you have to be careful about how you ask for it. A committee of employees gathering together to come up with suggestions or ideas sounds like good participatory management—but it also can be considered a labor organization, especially if the purpose of the committee is to deal with employee grievances. Sure, it's not what you intended, you were thinking about getting some good suggestions, not worrying about labor relations rules and rights. These problems can be avoided if management participates on employee committees as an observer, or if the purpose of the committee is broader than just presenting employee grievances to management.

—NANCY L. O'NEILL, ESQ. OF THE NATIONAL LABOR AND EMPLOYMENT LAW FIRM JACKSON LEWIS

Knowing What You Can and Can't Influence as a Leader

L eaders in the US Army are trained to assess each leadership situation carefully before taking action. A key part of this assessment is to identify

- situational factors over which the leader has little or no influence, and
- situational factors over which the leader does have influence.

This is a powerful way to think about any situation. It focuses you on what you need to respond to (that's the stuff you can't influence) and it shows you what possible avenues you have available for responding (that's the stuff you can influence). It might only take 30 seconds to draw up these two lists. Try it next time before you take action. Sometimes a little planning can go a long way when it comes to taking appropriate leadership action.

What Works Best?

J anice Drescher, an experienced trainer and executive coach who has helped out with some of my client work in California, likes to ask an interesting question when she visits a new client and does interviews with managers and staff. She asks them, "What works well around here?"

It usually surprises people and they may take a while to come up with an answer (since they assume consultants and managers always want to focus on what's wrong rather than what's right).

What you hear when you ask this question is that certain processes or groups are working smoothly and well. You discover what the organization's greatest

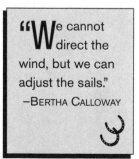

"We cannot direct the wind, but we can adjust the sails."
—BERTHA CALLOWAY

> It would be a shame to spend all your time fixing weaknesses and then discover you failed to capitalize on strengths!

strengths are. As a leader, you need to know where your strengths lie, if only to avoid making decisions that accidentally mess them up.

∪   ∪   ∪

Parting Thoughts

I suspect that less than one percent of our decisions as leaders will prove to have resounding impact when looked at a year or two later. Do we know which ones? Did we give them sufficient thought? Did we engage enough people in the decision-making process? Did we do enough research to minimize our risks?

Many managers dismiss such concerns with the comment that, while they may be remembered for just a few decisions, it's not possible to know which those are in advance. I don't agree. Decisions that change the direction of your group or that affect your ability to pursue your major goals are likely to be pretty important and visible in advance. Decisions about how to handle administrivia or where to go for lunch aren't. Yet the daily stuff of management tends to crowd out the big-picture issues until sometimes we find we have not thought about them at all, let alone taken the time to make a quality decision and involve those who must implement it.

One simple remedy is to vow to work on the most important item on your agenda first thing in the morning, and not switch to other items until you have made significant progress on it or run into a temporary roadblock that prevents you from doing more.

That way, all the less-important stuff has to wait while you work on the big stuff. Gives us a head start, doesn't it?

Decision-Making Checklist

This checklist highlights some of the best tips and techniques from the chapter.

✓ Don't make unimportant decisions. Save yourself for the ones that really matter!

✓ Don't make decisions your people can make just as well (or better).

✓ Be optimistic, but not overconfident. When there is uncertainty have a fallback option.

✓ Ask the people who will be affected by a decision for their input before deciding.

✓ If you have to make an unpopular decision, tell them *why*.

✓ Change your mind often. Circumstances often change!

✓ Never do something just because the competition does. They might be wrong.

✓ Give people a time limit for providing input on a decision.

✓ Ask people if they have any concerns or reservations. They might not tell you otherwise.

✓ Find other leaders you can talk to. Talking through a problem often helps.

✓ Make lists of the things you can and can't affect, then work with those you can.

✓ Preserve the best practices of your organization. Don't accidentally throw out the baby with the bath water!

✓ Decide what your most important decision is and work on it first thing in the morning, forcing the less important questions and chores to wait.

10

Development

Every winning horse has a great trainer who thinks about tomorrow's challenges while the horse is winning races today. Winning horses spend a lot of time in training—their success is no accident! Winning managers develop their organization's talent, too. In doing so, they may want to remember that some horses are natural runners, others jump high or pull hard or are good on the trail. Similarly, each person in an organization has unique strengths and we do our best when we recognize and develop them fully. The seeds of tomorrow's successes must be planted today.

> Winning horses need to train a lot. Prepare for tomorrow's races today!

"Treat people as if they were what they ought to be, and you help them to become what they are capable of being."

—GOETHE

Development is an essential part of turning on and tuning up any organization, team, or group for two reasons. First, people are only at their best when they are growing and developing, personally and professionally. Work needs to be a growth experience in order for the workers to achieve peak performances.

Second, you need all the help you can get, and your organization will need more and better people in the future. Think about the basic trends in our economy for a moment. Each year there are more people, more companies, more technologies, more products for sale, more ideas, more facts. They say that some of these factors— information, for example—are actually growing exponentially, which is faster than *I* can cope with, that's for sure!

Common sense says that each generation must be better and smarter than the previous one. Interestingly, in modern times IQs have been rising about 20 points with each generation (it's called the Flynn Effect if you want to sound like *your* IQ is rising too). I don't know how IQs keep going up, but I can certainly see why they *need* to.

Within our organizations, we need to raise our business IQs far more quickly than that, since each "generation" is far shorter (consider the fact that employees switch jobs every few years). If you think you might need people to lead a team, step up to a

A Personnel Decisions International survey revealed that less than a quarter of U.S. high-tech employees had individual development plans, but that more than 80 percent said they'd be more likely to stick with their current employer if they had a development plan and more feedback about their performance.

Can you have a learning organization without learning *people*?

promote, or handle a tough new project next year, you have to ask yourself where you are going to find them. The simplest answer is, under your own nose. It is usually easier to develop your own talent than to have to go out and compete for it on the open market.

But all that is beside the point, because in truth we need better, smarter employees *right now*. Anything leaders can do to foster a spirit of learning and development today is likely to begin paying off tomorrow. For a while there it was faddishly popular to talk about building a "learning organization." This is a nice ideal, but I suspect that in reality learning organizations are simply made up of learning people. Are your people learning?

I'm reminded of the old saying, "If you're not growing you're dying." There is something to this notion that life itself is a learning process, and that to fully enliven our people we must as leaders nurture their growth and development, just as we would the growth of any living being.

One thing I know for sure is that in every organization that really seems to "have it" you find that the people are growing and learning and developing just as fast as their organization, if not faster. Here are some of the ways that we as leaders can make this happen in our own workplaces.

U   U   U

Measure and Track Employee Development Efforts

How much time and effort do you or other managers in your organization put into developing star performers? If we did a careful time analysis of your daily schedule, we might find the amount of time spent on employee coaching and development is under 1 percent, since that is pretty typical in today's busy workplaces. The only way to improve that number is to start tracking it. How can you manage something you aren't aware of?

That's what they did at Sears Credit. Now front-line supervisors and managers are not only encouraged to focus on employee development—they are expected to keep a log of their development efforts and to be able to show that they put 80 percent of their time into development-related activities. Their new job definition is to be helping associates develop their skills instead of trying to do the work themselves.

Make Sure Opportunity Knocks Often for Your Employees

Opportunities are powerful motivators—whether they are short-term opportunities to tackle an interesting challenge in your work, or long-term opportunities to grow and develop in your career. Yet in the hustle and bustle of daily work it can be hard for leaders to make sure everyone is aware of and pursuing appropriate opportunities. Research suggests that employees often lose commitment and leave a job because they think they *lack* opportunities there. Managers need to make a better effort to keep everybody "opportunity focused."

One approach is exemplified by First USA Bank's Opportunity Knocks program. Employees participating in the program attended career development

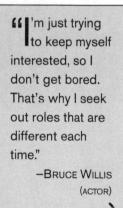

"I'm just trying to keep myself interested, so I don't get bored. That's why I seek out roles that are different each time."

—BRUCE WILLIS
(ACTOR)

> **E**mployees often lose commit-ment and leave a job because they think they lack opportunities. How could we prevent this from happening?

sessions to explore their interests and strengths and define career development goals, and then they worked with their managers to gain additional experience and training to help them achieve those goals. Promotion and retention rates were dramatically higher than normal for participants in the program and an internal survey showed significant increases in employee satisfaction.

You might assume that your employees can figure out how to grow on their own, but this case shows that people often need guidance to help identify their next steps and assistance in preparing for them as well.

Offer Opportunities, not Knocks

There is a fine line between opportunities and problems. In fact, one person's exciting opportunity can be another's high-stress crisis. You want to be careful as a leader not to overload employees with opportunities and create more stress than motivation by accident. But it can be hard to know whether someone is truly enthusiastic about a new assignment or challenge—or secretly concerned and distressed. In fact, as long as you offer opportunities on a yes/no basis, many more people will say yes than probably should have because they will assume you expect them to. To get around this, offer a range of options for their involvement, including a low-key easy option, at least one mid-level option, and finally a full-blown challenge that would be a big step for them. Then ask which one they'd prefer. Give them a few days to answer if they need it. That way, people will tend to find their right level of challenge.

For instance, imagine you are setting up a project team to prepare plans for moving into a new facility. Typically, the leader might assign people to such a team or more likely ask for volunteers. But what can you do to offer a range of challenges instead of just an either-or choice? Here are some ways to break up the project into roles that involve a range of effort and challenge levels.

- Define some of the team roles in terms of how much effort and difficulty they involve. For instance, maybe the central planning roles are more difficult and time-consuming than the supporting research roles. If you develop simple role descriptions (a bit like posting a new job opening) it is easier for employees to find an appropriate fit.
- Create supporting roles as well as central ones. For instance, maybe a core team of three people could handle the move, getting help in specific areas from several supporting teams that the core team coordinates. Make sure everyone knows that the supporting teams are expected to put less time and effort in than the core team and people will tend to self-select for the level of commitment that is most appropriate for them right now.

As the leader, you can make up the rules to many of the games your people play. There is no reason for any of them to sit on the sidelines—or to be on the field in a role they are not prepared to handle. When you start designing tasks and opportunities so as to offer a range of challenges, you'll get more employees productively engaged with their work.

> "What is motivational to one person isn't motivational to another."
> —CRYSTAL JACKSON, PERSONNEL MANAGER, COMPANION LIFE INSURANCE

>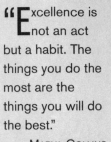
>
> "**E**xcellence is not an act but a habit. The things you do the most are the things you will do the best."
>
> —MARVA COLLINS

Puzzle Contests

One company has a number of crossword puzzle fanatics in it. Periodically they get multiple copies of the daily newspaper, hand out the crossword puzzle to volunteer teams of employees, and see which team can complete it accurately first. It creates a fun rivalry and employees enjoy it—and also gain confidence in this specific skill, which tends to spill over to their attitude toward work as well. This is, incidentally, also a good way to get employees sharing knowledge and cooperating, so it's a good rapport builder for work groups or teams as well.

The Gift of Choice

Do you have any idea how many aspects of working life are controlled by red tape, regulations, or requirements in your workplace? Most managers operate with a lot more latitude than their employees do. It makes a difference in their attitude and approach to work—a big difference. When it comes to the top executive or the business owner, the amount of freedom they have is dramatically more than their employees. They are permitted to decide what they think they ought to do each day, and even when, where, and how to do it. The average employee is treated like a felon by comparison—their employers do not trust them in the least. Yet they are expected to act like owners themselves, to care, to take initiative, and take the company's problems and challenges to heart.

It's a testament to the integrity of the average employee that they continue to do a decent job even when treated like they cannot be trusted. While we could gripe and grumble all day about how terrible it is to have tight controls that signal distrust of employees, the truth is that this presents a remarkable opportunity for us, rather than a problem. Because if you as a leader give employees a little more control than they are used to and show them you trust them more than most managers do, they will respond to this humane treatment surprisingly well. It doesn't take much water to make a desert bloom.

Help Employees Net Meaningful Volunteer Opportunities

Encouraging employees to do volunteer work of their choice is not only good for society but very good for the company because of the powerful harvest of positive feelings and self-confidence that comes from helping others. Employees who make a difference and achieve some success in their volunteering are more likely to have high morale and take initiative in their jobs—and develop more rapidly into promotable leaders. Some companies have a real tradition of volunteering and encourage employees to get out there and give their time and expertise. Carlson Cos., the travel and entertainment conglomerate, has taken this idea to a wonderful new level for its headquarters staff by creating a Web site on which Minneapolis-area nonprofits can post their needs. Employees use the site to find causes they are excited about and get in touch with the organizations of their choice. It's like a giant electronic billboard and it is increasing the amount of volunteering done by Carlson employees (who, if you recall, call themselves colleagues). This should in turn benefit the company in the long run.

Trust needs to be an action, not just an attitude. It is not enough to avoid open displays of mistrust. To motivate great performances, you need to seek out ways of giving employees options—showing them time and again that you trust them to make good choices.

> **"The greatest employee development comes from managers taking time to develop employees through mentoring, assigning interesting projects, and identifying improvement areas."**
>
> —MICHAEL SIMPSON, WATSON WYATT WORLDWIDE (IN *HR MAGAZINE*, MAY, 2001)

If you don't have the programming resources to build something similar from scratch, there are many easier ways that might work almost as well. You could add a "Volunteer Positions" section to your company newsletter and send out a press release announcing that you'll publish ads from nonprofits in your area (you might want to limit them to 25 words if you get too many). You could try to partner with a local umbrella organization such as a Rotary or Chamber group or United Way to create a community-wide shared Web site that does the same thing at lower cost to you.

Support the Charities Employees Work For

Levi Strauss and a number of other companies have made a policy of putting some of their charitable contributions toward organizations that employees volunteer for. If you as a business leader have any discretion over donations made by the organization, consider dividing them up among charities that employees are involved in. It shows respect for their initiative and supports a cause of importance to them.

Brain Power

Web Industries lets assembly-line workers take reading breaks and makes thought-provoking publications available for them. If you want your employees to think, this is a good way to encourage some mental calisthenics.

Rediscovering the Career Ladder

Kingfisher PLC, one of Europe's leading retailers, recognized that younger employees did not share the

LEGAL PERSPECTIVE

Favoritism

It is important to avoid the appearance of favoritism. Favoritism raises the question of why some people are not getting as favorable treatment as others—which can easily turn into complaints of discrimination. If an employee gets special treatment because of good performance, make sure the reason is clearly documented. Similarly, if employees do not qualify for some special treatment (it could even be a reward designed to motivate), then make sure their lack of the special treatment is clearly linked to their lack of the required performance.

Performance reviews help provide clear documentation to avoid the appearance of favoritism. Also, when giving verbal praise to superior performers, back it up with something in writing. The employee appreciates it when a good comment on performance is added to his or her personnel file, and this also provides documentation for any special treatment you might give to reward the performance.

—NANCY L. O'NEILL, ESQ. OF THE NATIONAL LABOR AND EMPLOYMENT LAW FIRM JACKSON LEWIS

commitment and loyalty of the senior managers, and decided that the lack of a clear career path within the company was partly responsible. To address this, the company launched what it calls The Kingfisher Management Development Scheme (or KMDS for those who don't think an initiative is real until it has an acronym). This initiative included a commitment to fill 80 percent of senior management positions internally, and also a promise to new hires with management potential that they would be advanced to senior management in seven to ten years. Having made these commitments, the company had to

> "Empowerment comes from teaching others things they can do to become less dependent on you."
> —KEN BLANCHARD, JOHN P. CARLOS, AND ALAN RANDOLPH, IN *EMPOWERMENT TAKES MORE THAN A MINUTE* (BERRETT-KOEHLER, 2001)

Seattle Goodwill Industries and Bank of America co-run an innovative four-week course to prepare unemployed welfare recipients for positions such as vault processors, account services clerks, and customer service operators (65 of the first 66 trainees have successfully moved into jobs at the bank).

rethink its approach to employee development and make sure internal candidates for management received plenty of training and exposure to different aspects of the operation.

Ask Talented Employees to Teach Their Crafts

The interesting thing about performance is that people who are good at doing one thing are more likely to want to do other things well too. Encouraging employees to develop and share any special interests is an investment in excellence, not just in their specific area of interest but in the workplace in general. One way to encourage employee excellence and share its motivating benefits is to invite employees with special skills or interests to put on workshops for other employees.

Be Careful Not to Favor the Angry

Most leaders would prefer not to promote impatient people who have bad tempers. Do we want angry team leaders and supervisors? Probably not, nor do the employees who would have to put up with their tirades. But recent research (by Larissa Z. Tiedens of Stanford Graduate School of Business) reveals that most people have a hidden bias that leads them to promote people who express their anger visibly. In their studies people were given choices of who to promote to a position of authority—and tended to choose the candidates who lost their tempers most often.

Why this strange bias toward promoting people with poor anger control? It might be because leaders in authoritative organizations are traditionally the ones who are permitted to show their anger, so we have come to associate displays of anger with high status. Whatever the reason, this is a subconscious bias worth avoiding. Be careful not to assume someone is leadership material just because they are bossy and get mad at others. In reality, such people may make poor leaders and are more likely to upset or demotivate their followers than those who are more emotionally mature.

Offer Community Service Awards

The S.C. Johnson Company, a private maker of name-brand cleaning, yard care, and self-care products, has a long tradition of community service. Employees contribute their time and expertise to many charities, gaining valuable leadership experience and increasing their pride in the company in the process. To encourage community service, the company offers annual Community Service Awards (a top award and sometimes multiple honorable mentions). The winner gets to donate $5,000 in company money to the charity of his or her choice and honorable mention recipients get to donate $500. Recipients also receive engraved crystal sculptures and recognition through an award ceremony, press release, and front-page coverage in the company's weekly newsletter. To help others follow the winners' lead, the company has a Community Leadership Department that can match employees with charities looking for assistance. (Story collected from SCJ while consulting to them, January, 2001, Racine, Wisconsin.)

Offer Lunch Learning?

Colle & McVoy, Inc., an ad agency in Bloomington, Minnesota, operates a "lunch hour campus" in

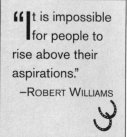

"It is impossible for people to rise above their aspirations."
—ROBERT WILLIAMS

Just how well do your employees know each other?

which brief courses are offered to employees once a week. New hires go through nine weeks of training in this format. (This is a great way to slip some continuous learning into busy schedules! An interesting variation on this idea would be to ask employees to teach some of the lunch lectures instead of just attend them.)

Leading by Offering New Perspectives

Some managers make a point of bringing new ideas and perspectives to their employees. For example, the leaders at Tapemark, a midwestern manufacturer, invited a psychologist to give a series of seminars for factory workers called "Wholehearted Living and Leadership," which addressed quality-of-life topics such as motivation, optimism, and thankfulness. Now that's not your average factory training session, is it?

Leading the Way with Personal Development Planning

Manufacturer Tapemark of St. Paul, Minnesota also sets up meetings for each employee with their supervisor and a human resources staffer to create personal development plans. This gets not only the supervisor but also the employee thinking about how to take advantage of growth opportunities. For example, some employees shadow others on the job in order to learn a new skill.

Playing Together Pays Off

HealthEast sponsors Employee Activity Clubs at its facilities to encourage employees to get involved in fun and challenging activities outside of work.

Making Good Citizenship a Management Responsibility

Managers of individual Loews Hotels are encouraged to find a local charity to support. One hotel donates food and any extra supplies to the homeless through a local church. Another hotel focuses on keeping a stretch of nearby beach clean and free of litter. The managers of each hotel encourage employee participation in these programs.

Delegate Quick Successes

If you give people confidence-building tasks, you help people make a habit of success. You can use this technique whenever someone seems to need a boost in order to be "turned on" and stretching for high performance. Also whenever there are minor things that you don't need to do yourself and could delegate to someone.

Ask someone to do something simple with a short-term, visible result and then make sure they succeed and are recognized (thanked) for it. Some examples might be:

- In the last meeting we decided to get some plants for the common areas. Could you take charge of selecting appropriate plants and finding someone to deliver them?
- This customer has some questions I know you can answer. Do you mind talking to them for a couple of minutes?
- That new employee hasn't used the _____ system before. Can you take a minute to show her how to get access to it?

"Common sense tells us that success makes people optimistic. But...the arrow goes in the opposite direction as well. Optimistic people become successes. In school, on the playing field, and at work, the optimistic individual makes the most of his talent."

—MARTIN E. P. SELIGMAN, PH.D (AUTHOR OF *LEARNED OPTIMISM*)

> **I** tell our
> employees, 'If
> you don't grow,
> then you go.' We,
> like any other
> company, cannot
> afford to have
> people who are
> not continuing to
> grow and learn."
> –KEN BLANCHARD

- I've got to make a purchase decision and I know you are familiar with this kind of _____. Can you give me a recommendation?

(From *1:1 Leadership*, Alexander Hiam & Associates)

Math Puzzles

One manager, believing that logic and math skills are important, brings in a weekly puzzle and posts it for employees. It might be a clever word puzzle, a short who-done-it, or some other sort of logic-oriented problem. Entries are put in a sealed box, and at the end of the week the box is shaken and a drawing is held. The first correct answer to come out of the box receives a prize. Nothing like encouraging the kind of skills you want your employees to have, is there?

Parting Thoughts

Consulting firm Watson Wyatt Worldwide found in a study of 1,000 firms that those investing more in leadership development also showed statistically better shareholder return, profits, and sales growth. (From the report: *Leadership in the Global Economy*)

According to a retention study done at insurance firm The Hartford, employees want "managers who are really interested in their development and in mentoring and coaching them," according to John Madigan, vice president of Human Resources (quoted in *HR Magazine*, May 2001). That at least is what employees complained about when they quit their jobs. Now that managers know this is a priority they provide a lot more guidance and advice about how to gain skills and advance careers.

Development Checklist

This checklist highlights some of the best tips and techniques from the chapter.

- ✓ Look within your group for future leaders.
- ✓ Help your employees find growth opportunities in their work.
- ✓ Create a range of roles from low to high challenge in order to accommodate each individual's readiness for change.
- ✓ Practice problem-solving and change so people are ready to handle the real thing.
- ✓ Find as many ways as possible to give your people control over their work.
- ✓ Encourage employees to do meaningful volunteer work in their community; this not only helps others but gives the employees more strength and initiative.
- ✓ Schedule reading breaks.
- ✓ Never play blame games. They prevent learning and improvement.
- ✓ Ask talented employees to teach their crafts and skills to others.
- ✓ Give employees short assignments they can master in order to help them make a habit of success.
- ✓ Be optimistic and encourage positive thinking in others—it leads the way to success.
- ✓ Train your horse! The business that practices, improves.

About the Author

Alex is an enthusiastic teacher and student of business leadership, a topic he has addressed in his consulting, research and writing for two decades. He began this work as a planner for executives in the '80s (both consulting and serving in management). His first book to explore leadership and performance was *The Vest Pocket CEO: Decision-Making Tools for Executives* (Prentice Hall, 1990), in which he wrote about participatory decision-making, nonfinancial motivators, and other foundational issues of modern leadership. He also explored leadership in turnarounds in his 1992 book, *Closing the Quality Gap: Lessons from America's Leading Companies* (written with The Conference Board).

In 1996, Alex addressed leadership and management issues in new and high-growth firms in *The Entrepreneur's Complete Sourcebook* after consulting to various Silicon Valley management teams. In 1997 his *Portable Conference on Change Management* assembled original contributions from top leaders and other experts on transitions. In *The Manager's Pocket Guide to Creativity* (1998), he extended his work to the leadership of innovative teams and organizations.

Hiam's work on generating initiative in the workplace is described in *Motivating & Rewarding Employees: New and Better Ways to Inspire Your People* (1999), and of course this book, *Making Horses Drink: How to Lead & Succeed in Business*. A detailed primer of his approach to motivational leadership based on his workshops and courses is also under development and will be released by the American Management Association under the title, *Motivational Management*. He also is a columnist on management issues for *Entrepreneur*.

Alex has provided leadership development and training for managers at AT&T, Eaton, Ford, GM, Kellogg's, The U.S. Postal Service, Dash.com, S.C. Johnson & Sons, Young & Rubicam, Linkage, McLeod USA, Association of Independent Trust Companies, and HealthEast and has also helped trained federal employees from the Navy, the FBI, the USDA, the U.S. Senate, and other organizations. He has also spoken about his work to professional groups such as the National Association for Employee Recognition and the American Society for Training and Development.

Alex received his AB in anthropology from Harvard and his MBA in strategic planning from U.C. Berkeley and at one point in his career served on the faculty of the School of Business at U. Mass Amherst. He maintains offices in Amherst, Massachusetts and San Francisco, and has served on the boards of the Northern California Human Resources Association and various nonprofits and foundations. Alex also tries to apply his interest in leadership and motivation to his volunteer work as a youth soccer coach and his role as a parent of three children.

Professional Products and Services

Alexander Hiam & Associates helps business leaders achieve above-the-curve performance through original training materials, workshops, and keynote addresses. The firm designs and delivers unique courses on leadership, conflict management, and employee motivation, and publishes a broad selection of tools and materials for other trainers as well (including assessment tools, training courses and workbooks, and educational games and case histories).

More information about Alex's publications and his firm's products and services can be found at streetwisemotivation.com or alexhiam.com, and you may write for a training materials, catalog, or event bookings to Alexander Hiam & Associates, 295 Amity Street, Amherst, MA 01002, call 413-549-6100, or visit www.alexhiam.com for more information.

Profile of Leadership Opportunities

This is an assessment tool (questionnaire) used by leaders in workshops or used in surveys of their employees to identify which of the ten leadership domains covered in the chapters of this book is the most likely to yield enhanced results. It can be used to design a consultation, coaching session, or course around the content of *Making Horses Drink*. Let us know if you would like to see a sample by contacting the author's firm at the above address or e-address.

Jackson Lewis

For over 40 years, Jackson Lewis has placed a high premium on preventive strategies and positive solutions in the practice of workplace law. We partner with employers to devise policies and procedures promoting constructive employee relations and limiting disputes.

When complaints arise, we work with clients to take incisive action to effect solutions that minimize costs and maximize results. Whether we are counseling on legal compliance or litigating a complex case, we help our clients achieve their business goals and promote an issue-free work environment.

With offices in major cities throughout the U.S., Jackson Lewis combines a national perspective with an awareness of local business environments. Our clients represent a wide range of public and private businesses and nonprofit institutions. We are experienced in all aspects of workplace law, including:

- employment litigation
- affirmative action
- race, gender, and age discrimination
- sexual harassment
- preventive labor relations
- union avoidance
- strikes
- collective bargaining
- grievance arbitration
- employee leaves
- pension and benefit administration
- immigration
- wage and hour
- independent contractors and contingent workers
- occupational safety and health

- substance abuse and drug testing
- employee privacy
- disability rights
- workplace violence
- restrictive covenants and non-compete agreements
- alternative dispute resolution

For more information about the firm, please visit our Web site, www.jacksonlewis.com; or you may contact Nancy O'Neill, at 415-394-9400, oneilln@jacksonlewis.com.

The author's firm provides
workshops and training
based on this book.

Visit
www.alexhiam.com
for more information.

Index